LEARNING TO WALK ALONE

Learning to
Walk Alone

Personal Reflections on a Time of Grief

Ingrid Trobisch

VINE
BOOKS

Servant Books
Ann Arbor, Michigan

Vine Books is an imprint of Servant Publication designed
to serve Evangelical Christians.

Published by Servant Books
P.O. Box 8617
Ann Arbor, Michigan 48107

Cover photo H. Armstrong Roberts
Book design by John B. Leidy

Printed in the United States of America
ISBN 0-89283-301-7

    86 87 88 89 90 10 9 8 7 6 5 4 3 2

Library of Congress Cataloging in Publication Data

Trobisch, Ingrid Hult.
   Learning to walk alone.

   1. Bereavement—Religious aspects—Christianity.
2. Consolation. 3. Trobisch, Ingrid Hult.   I. Title.
BV4908.T76 1985   248.8'6   85-2068
ISBN 0-89283-301-7

To my children
Who so courageously coped
with their father's death
and their mother's rebirth.

And to my "circle of lovers"
who taught me how to swim
in the sea of grief.

Contents

Our wedding day in Mannheim with Pastor Fuchs.

Preface

THIS BOOK IS FOR WIDOWS and widowers. It is for those who are alone because of separation or divorce, or because they have never married. I also wrote it for everyone who knew my husband and me, and who asked at the funeral, "What will happen to Ingrid now that Walter is gone?" It is my personal pilgrimage as I learn to walk alone again.

I want to share my experiences, too, with those who are not yet alone. It is a fact that the majority of women will outlive their husbands. Shouldn't they be prepared for widowhood, just as we prepare pregnant couples for childbirth? This book is written for men as well as women. It can be even harder for a man to cope with loneliness. Often he is tempted to rush into another marriage or relationship before the wounds of losing his life partner have had time to heal from the inside out.

Much of what is recorded here will be from my journal—from the early stages of subjective grief to the "growing up" and objective acceptance of facing life alone. Both the grieving and healing processes take time. There is no shortcut through them. For me, private confession, dealing with guilt and remorse, followed by forgiveness and the healing of memories has been all-important.

The interaction of my family, each one grieving in a different way, is also a part of this account. I want to reveal the humanness of Walter Trobisch as a husband and father through statements and letters. Neither his children nor I want to memorialize him nor put him on a pedestal. I am sure he would have agreed with the handwritten note found on Martin Luther's deathbed: "We are all beggars." The longer we live, the more we recognize this truth.

Three weeks after Walter's death my pastor told me not to make a shrine of Walter's office or home, as some widows do. I couldn't. We had a very small home in the Austrian mountains, and it had to be rearranged to accommodate the living. We learned that after we had made order again, we could invite our Walter-Father back into our home, and there was merriness in all the corners, as during his lifetime.

I cannot explain the mysteries of death. I can only share my own experience and what my children and friends have taught me. In God's word we read: "There is rejoicing in heaven among the saints when sinners repent" and "we are surrounded by such a great cloud of witnesses." I like to think of that special "cheering squad" in heaven—for me it's composed of my grandmother, my father, Pastor Fuchs, Dr. Bovet, Walter—all those who blessed and encouraged me on earth and who are now in their heavenly home. "The communion of saints," "the prayers of all the saints," these words have new meaning to me now. I am beginning to understand what my pastor said after Walter's death: "You are separated from Walter physically, but you are closer than ever spiritually."

My final prayer for this book is that it will be a helpful baring of the soul. I do not wish to wave the flag of grief, as some may do in order to get attention. But I have learned that only that which comes from the heart will reach the heart. Therefore, I pray that it will be a heart-book, helping husbands to love and understand their wives, and wives to learn to understand their husbands. May it give courage to lonely pilgrims and show the importance of taking that first step in obedience.

> To and fro I am hurled.
>   I have to stay.
> Only obedience holds—
>   I haste, I rise,
> I do the thing he saith.
>
> —George MacDonald

Father will always remain in my memory as a "traveler."
Especially when I was younger, it was one of the hardest
things for me to see him and Mother leave. But in the
moment we were all back together again it seemed as if all
the waiting, all the longing and the feeling of being left
behind was completely blotted out. I can well remember
how he asked me once what would make me happy. I said,
"The coming back home." His answer: "How can you
come back home if you have not been away from home?"

Stephen Trobisch
Freshman at the University of Vienna

Walter and I in Cameroun in 1953.

ONE

Coming Back Home

W ALTER AND I HAD JUST RETURNED from a trip around the world. We had been gone for almost three months. The day we left our little home in the foothills of the Austrian mountains, I asked Walter what he was looking forward to most during the long trip that was to take us to assignments in Indonesia, New Guinea, Australia, and the United States. Walter replied, "What I'm looking forward to most is the day I can walk over this threshold again."

We arrived home safely on the first of October, just in time to celebrate the engagement of our oldest son, Daniel. Betty and Daniel were both graduate students in Salzburg and were planning to be married in a few months.

Ruth, our youngest daughter, was in her last year of high school, also in Salzburg. The day after we returned home, she urged Walter to hike with her in the mountains. He readily agreed. An early first frost had transformed the wonderful old trees into a blaze of color and the mountain air was crisp and refreshing. Later, Ruth expressed her surprise at how often Walter had stopped along the way in order to catch his breath, contrary to his usual steady, but energetic pace.

While father and daughter were climbing that day, I had a chance to review some of the "mountains" Walter and I had climbed together since we had met thirty years ago in the halls of Augustana College, in Rock Island, Illinois, where we were both doing graduate work.

Pastor William Berg had told me about the arrival of this German exchange student who had already graduated from the University of Heidelberg's Department of Theology. Walter Trobisch had come on a scholarship to Augustana Seminary. He wanted to learn about the practical application of theology in American congregations. Pastor Berg told me that the student from abroad had many questions. He was especially curious to know more about American young women and what they were thinking. Reluctantly, I promised my pastor I would try to find time to talk to Herr Trobisch.

But there had been little time. My commissioning service was to be held in a couple of months. I was called to go to French Cameroun, in Africa, as a missionary teacher. Before that time, I would have to spend at least eighteen months in Paris studying for my French teaching certificate. It was a step of faith, for the mission board's policy dictated that mission candidates needed to raise the funds for their own support.

I had almost forgotten about the German student until the evening of my commissioning. I knew that our pastor had invited him to be present, but how could I know what was taking place that evening in his heart?

Years later he told me: "As you were kneeling at the altar and the pastors were laying on their hands during the service of commissioning, I seemed to hear a voice, which said to me, 'The young woman whom you see there in front will someday become your wife.' I quickly put the thought aside, for I didn't see how our goals could ever be the same. You were headed for Africa, and I wanted to be a missionary to my home church in Saxony, East Germany."

After the service, Walter asked for my address, so that we could exchange our newsletters. A few days later, I left Illinois to travel to Paris. A year later, as I was studying for my final exams, I received a letter of invitation from this young pastor, who was now serving a large congregation in Ludwigshafen, Germany. He asked if I would come and speak to his youth groups and tell them about my call to missions. I quickly declined his invitation, explaining that I was too busy with my studies and that I would soon be leaving for Africa. To my surprise, a few days later our French professor cancelled classes and announced a week of vacation to celebrate Mardi Gras and the beginning of Lent.

It became clear to me that I should spend those vacation days in Ludwigshafen. Taking all my courage in hand, I wrote another letter to Walter saying that I would be willing to visit him in Germany. *Willkommen!* was the prompt reply.

A few days later, I was seated on the back of a powerful German motorcycle, riding through the sleet and rain of a cold February day. Walter and I were on our way from

Ludwigshafen to Annweiler, a little village where one of his friends was conducting a series of meetings.

We were received by the local pastor's wife, who gave us steaming cups of tea and insisted that we soak our cold, wet feet in a tub of warm water. Walter, who was obviously enjoying himself, asked me what my friends would say if they could see me now.

Then we were taken to the Catholic church, where the whole community gathered together for these evangelistic meetings. (The Protestant church had been destroyed by American bombs and had not yet been rebuilt.) The people listened eagerly to the biblical teaching and testimonies of Pastor Herbert Fuchs and his team. Walter was part of that team. I can still see him wearing his gray motorcycle jacket in order to keep warm, for there was no heat in the church. He stood confidently in front of the audience which reacted with laughter and then careful attention as he told them a story and then gave a serious message.

At that time I understood very little German, but I could not mistake the clear inner voice which I heard, "This man, neither tall nor dignified, with his mischievous blue eyes, will be your husband." I gasped in disbelief. He looked so different than the man of my dreams. Yet he was the one I was to marry.

Years earlier, my father had said to me, after explaining the miracle of life: "Ingrid, you are not too young to pray for the one who will someday be your husband." I had listened to my father's advice. Whenever I developed friendships with young men, I would hear the quiet voice of the Lord saying: "No, he's not the one." Now, at the age of twenty-four, I heard for the first time: "This is the one I have chosen for you!" I couldn't sleep that night, so overwhelmed was I by the thought. I could only be silent, like Mary, "keeping all these things in my heart."

Two years later we were engaged. I was a missionary teacher in Cameroun, and he was a busy pastor in Germany. We were separated by continents, but we took to heart the words of Pastor Fuchs: "A Christian is one who can wait."

During that time I learned the ups and downs, not only of missionary life, but also of living as a single woman. Mail was delivered once a week to our lonely station. That little blue aerogram from Germany with Walter's strong and wise words filled my heart with joy, and I felt new energy to fulfill my ministry. I remember him writing: "Ingrid, let us love as if there would be no work. And then let us work as if there would be no love." Of two things I was very sure: first of all, I was a child of God; second, God was calling me to be the wife of Walter Trobisch.

On June 2, 1952, Pastor Fuchs married us in Mannheim, Germany. His text was taken from Isaiah 12: "With joy will you draw water out of the wells of salvation." We had it engraved in our wedding rings. My mother and Cliff and Lil Michelsen were the only Americans present that day. (There were 400 German guests, many of them from Walter's former congregation). Cliff spoke at the reception and told us that the secret of a good marriage was contained in a single word. If we could practice that word, then our frail little marriage boat, now leaving the sheltered haven, would be able to withstand the storms at sea. That word was "sharing."

We spent our honeymoon at a little hotel in the Black Forest. Every morning, after a leisurely breakfast, we sat across from each other at a picnic table in the little park and had our quiet time together. We read from the *Daily Texts,* the oldest and most widely used devotional book in the world, originated by Count Zinzendorf over 250 years ago. Walter's close friend, Wolfgang Caffier in East Germany, had been the editor of the German edition. After reading the text, Walter and I wrote down the answers to four questions which Martin Luther had once formulated for a friend: (1) What am I thankful for? (2) What troubles me? What do I need to repent and confess? (3) What is my special prayer request for this day? (4) What is my next step? What decisions do I have to make?

We shortened these four questions to four words: *thanks, sorrows, prayers,* and *action.* After taking a few minutes to listen to God's word in scripture and his voice, we wrote our thoughts down and then told each other what we had written. Only then did we take time to discuss and make decisions about our life together.

In this way we made the decision to go to Africa together. The door was closed for Walter to go back to serve in his home church in East Germany, and it was opened to Africa. During the first months of our marriage we lived in the same frugal one-room apartment in Ludwigshafen where Walter had lived as a single man. Then we went to Paris for a few months of concentrated language study. During that time, Walter received his letter of call from the Board of World Missions of the American Lutheran Church.

We arrived in Douala, Cameroun, on our first

wedding anniversary after a fourteen-day voyage. Our faithful motorcycle, which had taken us from Paris to Bordeaux, was our only means of transportation during the last part of our 1,000 mile trip inland. We were called to open a pioneer station in Tchollire, in the territory of King Rey Bouba in northern Cameroun.

Walter and I soon discovered how unheroic we were when we saw the four unfinished mud walls of what was to be our first home. Only the swollen banks of the Benoue River, over which there was no bridge, prevented us from making a hasty retreat. It took three long years of caring for the sick, teaching young men to read and write, and telling them the good news of God's love in Jesus Christ before the first little group of seven Christians was baptized.

On our third wedding anniversary we thanked God that we were to become parents. Katrine's birth, a few months later, was a time of great celebration, not only for us, but for all our African friends.

After our first furlough and the arrival of our oldest son, Daniel, we were asked to serve in Libamba at Cameroun Christian College, located in southern Cameroun. We spent six years there in what was dubbed by our colleagues the "Green Prison," surrounded as we were on all sides by the virgin forest, foreboding and impenetrable. These were happy years for me. I was absorbed in the fulfillment of being a wife and mother. We had two more sons, David and Stephen, and as a crowning answer to our prayers, our daughter Ruth.

In addition to teaching twenty hours of German (in French to Africans who had many different mother tongues), Walter was also the college chaplain. He found fulfillment as he saw fine young African students being formed. These would be the future leaders of Cameroun, a country which was suffering all the birth pangs of independence.

During these years in the "Green Prison," Walter began teaching classes on marriage for the older students. As a result of this experience, he wrote his first book, *I Loved a Girl*, a true story which contained the correspondence between him and one of his former students. These were the questions young Africans were asking about marriage. Before long, he began receiving an avalanche of reader's letters: "You answered the questions of Francois in your book. Now please answer mine."

In 1963, our home was transferred from Libamba, in the rain forest of equatorial Africa, to Lichtenberg, Austria, in the "Sound of Music" country. Lichtenberg was located less than an hour's drive from Salzburg, in the foothills of the Austrian Alps. Our neighbors consisted of four mountain farmers and their families. Living in this peaceful mountain hamlet allowed our children a liberty and freedom that would never have been possible in the city. For them it also meant a five-mile trek up and down the mountain in order to attend the village school each day.

For Walter, Lichtenberg was a place where he could work and write in peace. Laughingly, he would remark: "First I wrote *I Loved a Girl*, and then it wrote my life." Before long, the book had been translated into a score of African languages and every major European language.

We soon had to enlist help to answer all the letters that came to us from every part of the world. Requests to teach seminars on family life to church leaders in Africa and Asia followed. In order to do that, we needed more literature, and so we continued to write. The next step was to appoint a steering committee and form an umbrella organization. Co-workers were trained. Pastor Klaus Hess, one of our spiritual fathers, gave the name Family Life Mission to the new little tree whose branches began reaching out into all the world. We could only watch with astonishment and awe as we saw God at work in our midst.

These were just a few of the "mountains" I was thinking of that clear day early in October. I was also recalling the walk Walter and I had taken together in the beautiful autumn weather on the mountain overlooking Salzburg, just before our return to Lichtenberg. We stopped, full of wonder, before a linden tree whose perfect form and color made us think of the passage from a Psalm: "The righteous are like trees that grow beside a stream, that bear fruit at the right time, and whose leaves do not dry up" (Ps 1:3). We had meditated on this verse during our quiet time, and Walter had shared his thoughts after writing them down: "A tree rests, stands firm, drinks, supports, bears fruit, gives shelter, waits for the right time."

As we traveled from Salzburg to Lichtenberg, less than an hour's drive on the Autobahn, we stopped for coffee at Lake Mondsee. What a rare pleasure to have time, just the two of us, with no immediate assignments, just the joy of the weekend ahead of us, in which we planned to celebrate Ruth's eighteenth birthday, even though we were a month late. We drove up the mountain effortlessly. After the last serpentine curve, we were rewarded with what we called our "millionaire's view": Lichtenberg, where four farmers' homes clustered together, surrounded by their small fields, the valleys of the Salzkammergut, the brilliant blue of Lake Attersee, and the distant mountain ranges encircling us on three sides. We knew we were returning home, to one of the most beautiful spots in God's creation.

The next day we rested and breathed deeply. Walter took a sunbath on our little terrace while I baked Ruth's birthday cake and fixed our noon meal. "How I love to hear you making noises in the kitchen," he called out to me above the rattle of pots and pans. Three times that day we went for a walk—we needed to make up for all the weeks we had been gone. As the late afternoon shadows grew longer, we stopped to rest at our favorite bench. The clearness of that October air made even the distant mountains seem near enough to touch.

"I'm homesick," Walter said, "I don't know why. You are with me, and this is my favorite spot in the whole world. And yet I'm homesick."

After that, we went our separate ways for a couple of hours, so that Walter could read the letters on his desk which had accumulated in our absence. When I returned from my shopping trip to the nearby town of St. Georgen, I saw that our outgoing mail basket was full. Walter had answered many of the letters himself, addressing and stamping each one. That evening, after a supper of yogurt and raspberries from our own garden, he said to me with a sigh, "I'm not sure I will be able to answer every letter I get from now on. I'll give top priority to those young people who want to get right with God and find forgiveness. If the others or their parents who write to me will read my book, *Living with Unfulfilled Desires*, they will find my answers."

While I wrapped the little gifts we had collected for Ruth for her birthday celebration the next day, Walter read to me from a new book we had been given by one of our publishers, *Parents in Pain* by John White. It brought back to us some of the pain we had experienced as parents. "And yet," Walter said to me, "My heart is filled with deep thankfulness when I think of each child. Tomorrow I will write a letter to each one."

In the hours just before my birth in Ebolowa, Cameroun,
Father wrote the following lines in the journal Mother
had begun for me:
"We can only understand the exile. Our home remains
secret. The more we feel it, the more mysterious it becomes.
That which is foreign becomes home, and that which is
home becomes foreign to us. Messenger from home—you
are coming into your exile. And why? So that you may
become a messenger. Be a messenger, bring the home into
your exile! May you not get lost in your exile, but on the
joyful day of your return, find your way back home.
"Which day is greater—the day of birth or the day of
death? Why are both days necessary?
"We do not know. At one place only is there light—at
that place where God went the same way that you are
going today. We are never alone."

David Trobisch
Student of theology,
University of Heidelberg

Walter loved to hike in the mountains around our home.

TWO

Let the Deep Pain Hurt

"ALL IS WELL!" I THOUGHT, as I awoke the next morning. We have come back home. How luxurious to be in our own queen-size bed, which Walter had so lovingly ordered as a surprise for me when we moved to Europe.

In the German tradition, two beds are placed side by side, each one with its own mattress and its own feather bed. In between is a hard gap—they called it "visitor's gap" in Saxony, because the children had to sleep there whenever a visitor took over their beds. For the twenty-seven years of our marriage, we had coped with this "gap" when traveling in German-speaking Europe. But that day, I was glad to be in our own bed. I took it all in at a glance and thanked God for the familiar surroundings.

It was no surprise to see that Walter's pillow was empty. He had always been an early riser, slipping out of our room, often before dawn. He would go to his study and write, sometimes a couple of hours before we had breakfast together as a family. I was just the opposite, a night owl who hated to see the day end. In order to insure that we had precious time together before the demands of the day took over, he would prepare a pot of tea in the English tradition and bring it to my bedside. We would drink it and then read the watchword from the *Moravian Daily Texts*. Together, we would discuss our plans for the day, and then hand in hand we would pray, asking for God's strength and blessing.

I could hear the familiar sounds now on this Saturday, October 13, 1979. Walter was in the living room finishing up his morning exercise. I heard the rhythmic thud, thud, as his feet touched the floor. If weather permitted, he would usually go for a short morning run as well. He had reached his ideal weight goal, and at his last physical examination the doctor had congratulated him on his cholesterol count. At fifty-five, he was in good shape. He had never smoked (unless someone said it was a sin, and then he would do it ostentatiously to prove his freedom in Christ). Occasionally he would enjoy a glass of wine when there was reason to celebrate, but his happiness certainly did not depend on it.

Before long he opened our bedroom door. He was clad in his dark blue jogging suit, and his face was a little more flushed than usual. He greeted me when he saw that I was awake. "I'll bring our tea in a few minutes," he said. "I want to shave and bathe first." I waited contentedly. My clock radio had just clicked on, and I listened to the classical music that flowed gracefully from it. Today Ruth would be coming from Salzburg with Daniel and Betty. It would be a quiet family day, and I reveled in the thought of it. We were in our "place," and we were together.

Walter entered our room carrying the tea tray. He

placed it on the night table at my bedside and opened the curtains, letting in the full glory of an October morning on the Lichtenberg. Very matter-of-factly, he said to me in German: "My body is trying to tell me something, but I don't understand it." He had on his maroon dressing gown, which an African friend had given him years ago. His hair was neatly combed, and he was clean-shaven. He lay down on his side of the bed and propped himself up with his pillows while I poured his tea. I gave it to him and he held it for a moment, but then the cup began to tip. I called his name, but there was no answer—only his deep gasping for breath. I knelt at his bedside and tried mouth-to-mouth resuscitation, but there was no response. It all happened so quickly. I ran to the telephone and called our village doctor, who arrived within minutes. "It's too late," he said. "His heart has given out."

"It can't be true," I thought. "Walter spoke to me just a few minutes ago." The little white china teapot that he brought me was still warm. How could my husband of twenty-seven years pass so suddenly from this world to the next?

Disbelieving, I went to the door of our little house and called our neighbor Matthias and his wife Ernestine. Not long before, his mother had died in their house, surrounded by her children. Now death had invaded our home.

Matthias and Ernestine wept with me and then turned to the practical matters. They called the village pastor. I dialed the telephone numbers of the children: Stephen in Vienna, David in Heidelberg, and Katrine in Richmond, Virginia. I wanted to be the one to break the news to them myself. A strength not my own enabled me to do it. They all promised to come home as quickly as possible. Ruth was at school in Salzburg, so Matthias called her principal, who had to tell her the news of her father's sudden death. Friends told Daniel, who could not be reached by phone, and he would have to inform Betty.

I was numb with shock. The pain would come later. Now I had to be strong and make the right decisions. Matthias and Karl, another one of our neighbors, helped me dress Walter while his body was still warm. I picked out his favorite dark suit—his "Finland suit" he had called it, because he had gotten it for our trip to Finland five years earlier. Just yesterday I had come across his best white shirt in his drawer. "Put it in my small black suitcase," he had told me. "Then it's ready for my next trip." We chose his silver tie—the one he always wore for weddings and special celebrations.

Our Austrian pastor arrived. He prayed at Walter's bedside, together with all the neighbors from the four households on the Lichtenberg, who had come to grieve with me and offer their support. After that, I asked to be left alone in the room with my husband. I had no sense of time. Matthias had said he would go to the little town of St. Georgen, notify the funeral director, and pick out a simple pine coffin. I heard his wife in the kitchen preparing food for the children's arrival. As I knelt by Walter's bedside, I saw a change come over his face. It was a look of transfigured peace, almost as if he were smiling secretly. Heaven was very near in our little bedroom that October morning.

The watchword for that day, October 13, 1979, was

from Psalm 85:10, "Steadfast love and faithfulness will meet." And from Romans 12:12, "Rejoice in your hope, be patient in tribulation, be constant in prayer."

I couldn't grasp either one of them at the moment. I could only remember how two days earlier, during our quiet time, we had read the words, "I will turn their mourning into joy" (Jer 31:13) and the answering verse in the New Testament: "Blessed are those who mourn, for they shall be comforted" (Mt 5:4). At the time, my heart had been very sad about certain burdens God had entrusted to us. I had shared this feeling of great sadness with Walter. He listened patiently, and as I rested my head in his lap, he stroked my hair and said: "Ingrid, just let the deep pain hurt."

As I sat alone in my grief, I heard a car pull up in our gravel driveway and the next moment quick steps in the hallway. It was our third son, Stephen. He was a freshman at the University of Vienna, School of Engineering. His roommate Fritz had been with him when my call had come at 8:30 that morning. Fritz had driven Stephen's old car the 200 miles from Vienna at breakneck speed. They were the first ones to arrive. Stephen and I embraced in silence, and then he went into our room to weep over his father.

I put some hot water into the teapot, using the same leaves Walter had brewed our tea with earlier that morning, and then gave Stephen a drink of it. Before long, Daniel arrived with our youngest daughter, Ruth, whose eighteenth birthday we had planned to celebrate that day. Their grief was too deep for words. I served them some of the lukewarm tea and then went for a short walk with Stephen and Ruth. We walked down the same rutted mountain road that Walter and I had walked together the day before. I put my arms around them as we sat on the bench, and told them what I could remember of my last hours with their father.

It was late afternoon before David arrived with his fiancee, Vera, from Heidelberg. We all gathered at Walter's bedside. Daniel read the prayer of committal in our Lutheran hymnal, and we sang together in German: "Jesus, still lead on." We closed with our family prayer from Psalm 67:1-2: "May God be merciful to us and bless us! May his face shine on us, that the world might know your dominion and the nations know you save."

Then they came and took his body away—the last farewell from the home he loved so dearly. It was his final journey on this earth.

Five days later he was buried beside his mother in a little Alpine cemetery, in the shadow of the church where he had often preached during our fifteen years in Austria. The service was a celebration of his life. Inscribed on the family tombstone were the words, "In the morning, Jesus stood at the shore" (Jn 21:4).

It was the end of his pilgrimage on earth, but it was the beginning of my pilgrimage as a widow.

For my eighteenth birthday, on September 12, my father wrote me these words:

"Anxiety and tension will hover over you as you read the watchword for your birthday: Who can stand the day of His coming? (Mal 3:2) and God will not show mercy when He judges the man who has not been merciful (Jas 2:13). The urgency of this word will not make you relaxed and at ease. In German Barmherzigkeit *[mercy] means to carry with your heart. This is quite a life-program for your coming of age. I do not know what your future will look like. The secret of a fulfilled life, however, is to let yourself be carried by the heart of God. Only from there can you gain strength to carry others with your heart."*

Anxiety and tension have really hovered over these last days since Father's death, but we have all experienced again and again the mercy of God. I would like to take these words which Father wrote in my devotional book for 1979 as the motto for my future: "One step at a time! God shows us always just the next step."

Ruth Trobisch
Preparing for her university entrance
exams in Salzburg

Katrine and I at Walter's grave. The man on the left is Matthias, our next-door neighbor, with whom we had a very close relationship.

THREE

One Step at a Time

OCTOBER 22, 1979—"Today was a hard day. I had to go down the mountain, to the city hall in St. Georgen to get Walter's death certificate. It was a gray day. Life went on as usual, and people seemed to have forgotten the shock that passed through the little town just a few days earlier, when everyone first heard of my husband's death. But for me, life will never be the same. It was more than an amputation—losing an arm or a leg. I feel as if someone has taken an axe and split me from head to toe. Twenty-seven years of marriage have taken us around the world together—for over thirty years we had known beyond a doubt that we were called to be "one." Now they are at an end. Can I ever be whole again?

"One step at a time." Walter had written it in my *Daily Texts,* too, at the beginning of the year: "God shows us only the next step. He also comes to us in paths that were never there before." How thankful I was for my oldest daughter Katrine, who was going to stay with me for the next two weeks.

As soon as she arrived, after a long voyage across the

Atlantic, she took her baby, Virginia Ruth, and placed her on Walter's empty pillow. "Look, Mother, here is new life!" she said.

My sister Veda was still with me too. She had been the only one of my immediate family who had been able to come for the funeral. What would I have done without the quiet comfort of her presence? The night of the funeral, after caring for our out-of-town guests, we realized that we were still one bed short. Ruth joined Veda and me in the queen-size bed and we were strangely comforted.

But now the next step was to go on living. There were meals to be cooked and laundry to be done. Stephen had to return to his studies in Vienna. He said that he needed curtains for his room. We picked out the material together, and Veda helped me sew them. Even though my hands were trembling, like a patient returning home from the hospital after major surgery, it was good to do this practical deed for my son.

Katrine helped me read and sort the baskets of mail that arrived as the news of Walter's death went around the world. She knew I was concerned that our friends be informed of the details of his death and funeral. One evening, after she had nursed Virginia, she wrote a letter for me in German, and together we translated it into English. After including the tributes of her brothers and sister, she added her own:

"Father died in the morning. Jesus called him home at his most treasured time of the day. The eternal morning dawned. . . . Jesus may have prepared him a meal just as he did for his disciples that morning at the water's edge, and they are celebrating together. How Father liked to celebrate with us here on earth. Even out of the most trivial occasions, he could make feasts of joy.

"Father provided so well for us and was always concerned about how he could give us the best, both spiritually and physically. Our well-being was always more important to him than his own. One of the last things he did with Mother was to make decisions about the arrangements for our higher education. With tears in my eyes, I raise my head and wonder at how I could so often take his generosity for granted.

"Father put his whole soul into it when he planned for his family. He always tried to plan the right thing at the right time at the right place. Woe then, if things did not work out as planned! It's almost as if now my aching heart feels him making arrangements for us in heaven."

I could only continue to take one step after another, in the numbed determination of the bereaved. I had to sign Walter's letters, the ones he had dictated the day before he died, and which our German secretary had typed. He had also dictated a report to the mission board about his trip to New Guinea in August, 1979. It was in English, but our part-time English-speaking secretary said that she wouldn't be able to do it for me. It would hurt too much. So I did it myself. How clear and concise were his words on tape and how "natural" was his voice. To think that I shall never hear it again—telling of his love and laughing over our private jokes.

That night I dreamt that I was in Salzburg. I was walking alone, leaving our little apartment there to take the path along the Salzach River. I saw Walter, but I couldn't touch him. He walked ahead of me and I could only follow at a distance. Then I realized that someone was walking with him—one of those he had helped to come to the wholeness of Christ. In my heart came all the pain of knowing that I would never again be in his arms. Those whom he counseled and helped would have just as much of him now as I did.

Later, I shared my dream with Daniel. "You have all your good memories, Mother. And what you have had, no one can ever take away from you," he said comfortingly. A friend with whom I had studied in Paris and with whom we had worked in Cameroun wrote the same thought: "In order to lose, you have to have had something. If the Lord took away, it is also true that to do so, he had to have given in the first place."

Tears came at these thoughts, but they came from deep within, and they were good, cleansing tears. All I could do was to keep living—putting one foot in front of the other, for the sake of our children and for Family Life Mission, the tree which was just beginning to take root. I was untouched by much of what went on around me. Neither could I grasp any great spiritual truths—not even the words of comfort from well-meaning friends. All I could take hold of at that moment was the message of that short refrain from a song by the Jesuit Fathers in St. Louis:

Be not afraid!
   I go before you always.
Come, follow me,
   And I will give you rest.

November 4th, 1979—it was three weeks since Walter died. Katrine had to return to Richmond where her duties as a wife, mother of two daughters, and homemaker continued. Veda, a busy pastor's wife, left for Minneapolis a week before.

Walter and I had originally planned to spend this week attending a conference in Germany to celebrate the 250th anniversary of the first publication of the *Moravian Daily Texts*. Would I be strong enough to face people outside of my home and our mountain village? I had no courage to drive the 200 miles to Bad Boll in West Germany by myself. But Walter's best friend, Pastor Wolfgang Caffier from East Germany, was to be one of the main speakers. He wrote me: "Please do try to come, Ingrid. I know it will be hard, but it will be my only chance to see you, since I do not have a travel document to come to Austria on this trip."

Fortunately, David and Ruth offered to go with me. On the highway between Salzburg and Stuttgart I saw all the places where Walter and I used to stop and rest when we made this trip. I asked David to stop at one of our favorite places. We drank a cup of tea and then continued on our way. The deep pain was beginning to turn into tolerable pain.

Once we arrived at the conference center, I had to register at the desk. I wrote down my name, address, and passport number. But there was another blank to fill out: marital status. "Widow," I wrote. I felt like a spectator of myself. I didn't want to admit it, but I was a widow. And if I didn't believe it, I could just look at myself. I was dressed in black, as was the custom for a widow in

Europe. I thought, too, of what Walter had so often said to his counselees: "Your status can change from one day to the next—from being married to single and from being single to being married."

While I stood at the desk, Wolfgang Caffier entered the hotel lobby. His sensitive face betrayed his emotion, and he embraced me gently and then greeted Ruth and David. Walter and I had seen him just six months earlier, when he had invited us to Dresden for his sixtieth birthday celebration. What a wonderful time we had had there with him, his wife, three sons, and a host of friends. The festivities had lasted for three days, and during every free minute, Walter and Wolfgang were lost in deep conversation. Both of them had been born and educated in the city of Leipzig. Wolfgang, who was five years older than Walter, had been the leader of the Christian youth group in their neighborhood. Through his clear testimony and quiet discipling, Wolfgang had led Walter to faith. Wolfgang's mother was Jewish. Miraculously, both she and her family had escaped the Holocaust.

Now Wolfgang said to me: "You must be very quiet in your spirit, Ingrid. Through you, Walter became the man that he became. Because of you, he could work under a blessing, in freedom and in warmth." I was hesitant then to believe him, but at the same time his words gave me inner strength.

Before returning to Austria by train, I was invited to spend the weekend with Pastor and Mrs. Hess in Ottmaring. Klaus and Amalie Hess were both in their seventies and had been like parents to Walter and me. Their spiritual wisdom and love had often supported us in times of great need. Now I enjoyed the warmth of their home (Ruth and David had both returned to their classes), while they allowed me to pour out my heart. Their patience was great as I asked all the questions of remorse: "Why didn't I notice the signs that all was not well? Twice in the three weeks before his death, Walter had complained about knifelike stabs of pain in his heart. We had even made an appointment with the doctor on Monday—but he had died on Saturday. When he had bade my mother farewell in Springfield a few weeks ago, he had said 'I love you, Mother.' But his eyes were so far away. That last afternoon at home, he had said, 'I'm homesick, but for what?' Why hadn't I recognized any of the signs—the closeness of eternity?"

Then there were the guilt questions: "Why did I repeat to him a criticism that I knew would hurt without helping him? Why didn't I respond more warmly when he got up from his chair on that last evening and asked me, 'Do you think there is anyone who still loves me?' We were both suffering from battle fatigue and needed reassurance. How many times that last night of his life, instead of sleeping soundly as usual, had he reached out to me and said, 'Ingrid, I love you.' And drowsily I had thought: 'Why is he saying this so often tonight while at other times I have to wait days to hear it?'"

By Sunday afternoon I had shared all my accumulated guilt and pain. Pastor Hess said gently but firmly: "It is enough. We will place it all at the foot of the cross—at Jesus' feet." After we had prayed together, he pronounced the forgiveness of Christ and gave me a blessing which included each one of the children. I could weep cleansing tears as I sat in his wonderful, old winged armchair. I called it the "Father Chair," for that's just how I felt—as if I were seated there with my heavenly Father, being loved and comforted.

"Even though you are now separated from Walter physically," Pastor Hess said to me, "you are not separated spiritually. At the throne of grace in prayer and at the altar in holy communion, we are united with those who have died in Christ. We are surrounded by this great 'cloud of witnesses.' Go back to the Lichtenberg," he said, "but do not try to make it a shrine, as some widows do. It is only your earthly tent."

His words opened up a new dimension to me, and I was thankful for the wisdom of his experience and spiritual counsel. As I left on the train the next morning, he gave me a beautiful card to put in my Bible. On the back he and his wife had written in German: "Don't let yourself be tyrannized by anxiety and the stress of all that has to be done. Step by step, everything will become clear and fall into place. Heaven is very near. The way is being paved for something new. Peace and forgiveness surround you."

Jonathan Edwards was a colonial theologian and preacher who died in a very untimely way only a month after he became president of Princeton University. A few weeks after his death, his wife wrote the following in a letter to one of their children: "What shall I say? A holy and good God has covered us with a dark cloud. O that we may kiss the rod, and lay our hands on our mouths! The Lord has done it. He has made me adore his goodness that we had him so long. But my God lives, and He has my heart. O what a legacy my husband, and your father, has left to us! We are all given to God: and there I am and love to be."

My prayer for you, Ingrid, is that you might have the same courage Jonathan Edwards' wife did. May the Lord bless and comfort you.

Like great writers before him, Walter's works will live on. I've always been impressed by the fact that C.S. Lewis was read much more widely after his death than before.

Charles Colson

Walter with a group of his students at Libamba, Cameroun.

FOUR

The Legacy of Love

ONE MONTH AFTER WALTER'S DEATH, the letters were still pouring in from all parts of the world. He who could not weep since the hell he experienced as an eighteen-year-old infantry soldier in Stalingrad was wept for by many.

One of those who came to weep with us was Jean Banyolak, Walter's former student at Cameroun Christian College. He had decided to dedicate his life to work as a marriage counselor in Africa. Walter had been his mentor and had helped him receive professional training in Europe. Now he and his good wife, Ernestine, were pioneer African marriage counselors in Douala, Cameroun. Their ministry had already reached many parts of French-speaking West Africa.

Jean had received the news of Walter's death too late to attend his funeral—but now he came and sat with us in our grief, like Job's three friends. "Then they sat down with him . . . for seven days and nights. No one said anything to him because they saw he was suffering so much" (Job 2:13).

After the anesthesia of shock had worn off, the pain of

Walter's death seemed greater, not less. It was my African brother Jean who comforted me with his presence. Joseph Bayley described this kind of comfort after losing one of his sons,

> I was sitting, torn by grief. Someone came and talked to me of God's dealing, of why it happened, of hope beyond the grave. He talked constantly, he said things I knew were true.
>
> I was unmoved except to wish that he would go away. He finally did. Another came and sat beside me. He didn't talk. He didn't ask leading questions. He just sat beside me for an hour or more, listened when I said something, answered briefly, prayed simply, left.
>
> I was moved, I was comforted. I hated to see him go. (*The View from a Hearse,* David C. Cook, Elgin, Ill., 1973)

A young widow with two small children, who had lost her husband in a battle with leukemia, wrote to me to say that the first light comes in the darkness, in the jungle of grief, when one learns again to say "thanks" and to accept one's situation. "In acceptance lieth peace," says Amy Carmichael. To say thanks—not only for all that has been, but also for this time—could I do it?

One morning I felt as though the door opened and I was no longer in darkness. It was the first time since Walter's death, a month earlier, that I had slept so long and so peacefully. A yellow rose was placed on a tea tray on my night table. Had Walter been there? I felt comforted and strengthened. I didn't need to go on trying to be superhuman, stretching my already taut nerves. I had a "superhuman Companion," and it was because of his strength and love that I could go ahead. He would fill my empty hands. I stretched them out to him and walked toward the light of his presence.

The memory of that morning will always remain with me as a kind of turning point, enabling me to get on with the work of grief. (I found out later that Daniel had prepared the tray before he left for class that morning.)

I realized the importance of being allowed to mourn. Some doctors prescribe sedatives for their patients suffering from grief. But I was glad that mine seemed to know that mourning was therapeutic, a part of living. He knew that this lonely road had to be followed, one step at a time.

I could see the legacy of love that Walter had left me in our five children. Stephen, our youngest son, invited me to spend a few days with him in Vienna so that we could celebrate his father's birthday there. Vienna had always been Walter's favorite city—ever since he had arrived there as a wounded soldier from the Russian front. He had actually begun his theological studies at the University of Vienna. Last year he had spent a week alone in Vienna, where he had written the first act of a play—a play which was to highlight the biblical message on marriage. Would it ever be finished? I talked it over with Stephen as we sat in a Viennese cafe after hearing Haydn's "Creation." I felt sheltered and safe with my twenty-year-old son. I remember the words of our own marriage counselor, Dr. Bovet, who had said that it's not only the children who feel secure when they are with their mother, but the mother who feels secure when she is with her children.

A new dimension was opening up to me. I was learning to breathe deeply again and rest in God's love. All the love I would have liked to have given Walter, I could give to his children. I met my husband in each one of them and thanked God for the miracle of their lives.

Linda Getahun, a close friend and co-worker in Family Life Mission, wrote to me on November 29, on Walter's birthday: "I have heard it said that the mourner in his grief takes on the qualities of the deceased. During these past weeks, I've actually observed this in myself. If this phenomenon is true, Walter left even more blessing to us than we knew. When his children and spiritual children, in their grief, can take on some of his qualities and values, then they are enriched through the agony. Walter was just a wonderful human being. He was so rare, because he was so true."

This letter was echoed by another from one of Walter's counselees: "Ingrid, I don't want to hurt you, but I have to tell you that Walter is very close to me. He is around us in the cloud of witnesses that always accompanies us. I only knew him for three, short, intensive years. In a certain sense, I was healed through his ministry. If sometimes now I am tempted to be disobedient, then suddenly Walter stands beside me. His spirit influences my spirit. Indeed, through his death, he is almost a greater help to me, than alive. He surrounds me in Jesus Christ—rather, Jesus Christ surrounds me through Walter."

I was filled with awe when I read these thoughts from

people whom I loved and trusted, but I couldn't quite grasp them. Katrine had written in the letter to our friends: "Although Father died early, he left us much to remember him by. Through his letters and books we will be close to him. He made our lives and the lives of many others rich. We thank him."

Could anyone ever know the price those books had cost us and our marriage? Each one had to be "born"— just like a child, except that the pregnancy lasted much longer than nine months. I stood by and tried to protect Walter from the outside world while he was writing, and he had done the same for me. How many times we felt like throwing a manuscript on the fire! But we had learned: the greater the valley we had traversed before a book was finished, the greater the blessing of that book later on. Each time I worked on the final stages of Walter's manuscripts in English, I felt a deep and indescribable joy. Would I ever experience that joy again?

Six months before Walter's death, one of our friends, with tears in her eyes, said, "Walter, your ministry is just beginning."

He looked puzzled and asked her, "But how can that be? I'm already so tired. Perhaps you mean the books?" Now I remembered her words, spoken in quiet authority, and I thought of what Charles Colson had written me: "Walter's works will live on."

I was deeply touched and grateful for the words of our oldest son, Daniel, who had been his father's assistant for the past five years. Their teamwork had begun when they had traveled together, teaching seminars to couples in New Guinea for a six-week period. Now Daniel wrote to our friends: "Perhaps, as the eldest son, after having worked closely with him during these last years, I was the most conscious—even before his death—of the intellectual and spiritual inheritance of my father. A wonderful treasure of immeasurable wealth and a tremendous responsibility!

"That is why I daily pray for grace to be able to grow more intimately into union with our heavenly Father and Provider. One day I hope to pass on to my children and grandchildren that which my beloved father has given me."

In my mail was a card of condolence from a vineyard keeper in southern Germany: "Walter was a laborer in God's vineyard. He died in the middle of the grape harvest."

The idea of mourning *is extremely old and has been preserved in two of humanity's most ancient languages. The root meaning in Sanskrit is "to remember" and in Greek is "to care." Mourning is an emotion that results from the universal experience of loss—the way in which mourners adapt from what* was *to what* is. *To grieve (to be burdened by sorrow) and to be bereaved (to be robbed of someone or something precious) are part of—but only part of—the mourning process. Mourning is a process that takes you on the journey from where you were before loss to where you will be as you struggle to adapt to change in your life.*

Glen Davidson
Understanding Mourning

Daniel, Betty, and Michael Walter Trobisch, five years after Walter's death.

FIVE

Letting Go

I T WAS LATE FALL as I walked alone through the Mirabell Gardens in Salzburg. My heart was bleeding with every step. Walter loved this city and had even taken a course which licensed him as a tour guide. It was one of his favorite hobbies to take his friends through Salzburg and the "Sound of Music" country. He never tired of making new discoveries in this historic city.

Never again would I walk arm in arm with him there. Never again could I look forward to having a "date" with him in Salzburg as we had done regularly over the years. Even our children had known the signals when we needed time together. I remember Ruth telling me once, in all the wisdom of her eight years: "It's time you and Father went to Salzburg—just the two of you." She already knew that busy mothers and fathers need time for themselves, just to talk, without a tableful of family and guests listening in.

I had good memories, and I am thankful. One of my best friends had lost her husband, too, but not through death. He had decided he would feel more "fulfilled" by living with his secretary. Not yet forty, his wife had to cope with supporting and raising four children alone. She didn't even have a driver's license, and her self-image was close to zero. I watched her bravely overcome each hurdle. Because of her courage, she was an example to me as I faced my grief.

I soon learned that there is a great difference between being sad because I miss my partner (an expression of the love felt for the other one) and being sad because I'm feeling sorry for myself, which is nothing other than self-pity. If self-pity is one of the greatest poisons in a marital relationship, then it would seem even more dangerous to one who is learning to walk alone.

When I was tempted to self-pity, I had only to think of my own brave mother, who was only forty-four when my father died. She had ten children, the oldest of whom was in his freshman year of college at the time. Outside of a tiny widow's pension, she had no financial resources.

My situation was different. My youngest child would soon enter the university, and Walter had made provisions for the education of our children. If we all worked hard and were good stewards, we could manage.

After those first weeks were over and condolence letters no longer filled my mailbox each day, I began to feel relieved. Yet I longed and prayed for some kind of "declaration of love" each day that would bring healing to the raw edges of my heart. It's hard to speak words of comfort to yourself, just as it's hard to proclaim the gospel to yourself. We need a brother or sister to do it for us.

When I came home one day from a lonely walk through Salzburg, I found this letter from some Canadian friends: "How the Lord has blessed Walter! I weep when I think of him—and you. May he continue to bless you abundantly in your pain as Walter now knows you more fully and loves you more abundantly than when he was physically beside you.

"The Lord asked for similar surrender of your mother years ago, as he did also of his own mother. Continue on your way rejoicing and be assured that your witness to us all is supported by the love and prayers of the worldwide community to whom you have both given yourselves unreservedly. 'I am going to prepare a place for you—I will come back and take you to myself, so that you will be where I am. You know the way (Jn 14:2-4).'"

Everyone needs something to look forward to. One day a close friend of Katrine's invited me to a concert in Salzburg. Margaret made it a very special evening for me. Later, another young friend gave me a ticket to the Advent Singing at the Festival Hall, which I gratefully accepted. I was reminded of one of Walter's last written messages to me: "If you aren't good to yourself, how can you be good to others?"

A nurturing and supportive social network was absolutely essential for me at this stage of my grief. I felt like a small child, unable to reach out or even perceive the needs of others.

In spite of my aching heart, I knew it was right for Daniel and Betty to go ahead with their wedding plans for December 21. "What a good date they have chosen," a friend wrote. "This is the shortest day of the year, when darkness has the upper hand. Now light will come into your darkness, and each day the light will grow." Another friend wrote in response to the wedding invitation, "I was so sad when I thought of your little home on the Lichtenberg as a house of mourning. Once more there will be the happy sounds of the bride and bridegroom."

The evening before the wedding all five children were seated around our large round table in the kitchen. Many of their close friends were present also, and I counted sixteen young people relaxing and sharing. Pastor Hess, who was to perform the wedding ceremony the next day, said to me as he entered the room and sensed their contagious warmth, "Now I understand, Ingrid. This is Family Life Mission!"

One of our guests was a student from Hamburg who had driven almost a thousand miles to be with us. "I'm so grateful," he said, "just to sit at your table again. After a couple of days here I can soak up enough warmth to get me through a whole semester in the cold atmosphere of my university."

A couple of weeks before the wedding, Betty and I had gone to a retreat center in Salzburg. We had read and meditated on Isaiah 40: "Comfort ye, comfort ye, my people." At the close of the retreat we had participated in the Lord's Supper together. At that moment I experienced a certain closeness to Walter and began to understand what Pastor Hess had said: "You are now separated physically, but closer than ever spiritually."

In order to survive and grow out of my subjectivity, I knew that I needed to follow certain physical laws of health: a balanced diet, adequate fluid intake, daily exercise, and daily rest. Even if I could not sleep as well as

I had before my loss, I tried to maintain the same patterns of rest.

The day after our retreat, Betty and I went swimming together. "I knew when I saw you swimming again after father's death that you would be all right," one of my sons had said. For a few minutes I could "swim away" from all that was burdening me. At times I experienced clear guidance about my next step. The same was true when I went for a vigorous walk, often with a question in my heart. The answer would be clear when I returned home.

As I swam on that day, it became very clear to me that I should take off my wedding ring and give it to Betty. She and Daniel were to be married in two weeks, and he had asked, as the eldest son, whether he might have his father's ring. So, between laps, standing in the corner of the pool, I took off my ring and put it on her finger.

I *was* married to Walter Trobisch, and what I have had will not be taken away. But now death has parted us. I must let go in order to go forward.

No man can stay alive when nobody is waiting for him.
Everyone who returns from a long and difficult trip is
looking for someone waiting for him at the station or the
airport. Everyone wants to tell his story and share his
moments of pain and exhilaration with someone who
stayed home, waiting for him to come back.

Henri Nouwen
The Wounded Healer

At our home on the Lichtenberg.

SIX

Moving on Alone

I WAS IN FLIGHT ACROSS THE ATLANTIC—leaving one world for another. A memorial service for Walter had been planned at the Augustana Lutheran Church in downtown Minneapolis. Most of my family and many close friends would be there.

As my plane glided above the clouds, I thought about my eighty-one-year-old mother and the comfort that would come from seeing her again. Almost four decades ago, I had to relay the news of my father's death to her. He had died suddenly from a heart attack after a bout with malaria. He was buried the same day in the sweltering heat of Dar es Salaam, on the coast of East Africa. He loved his family so much, yet he had to be separated from them during his mission service in Tanzania. A few weeks later, we held a memorial service for him in his hometown in Nebraska.

I remember meeting my mother at the train station as she arrived from Springfield, Missouri, to come to Father's memorial service. I tried to comfort her. "Don't be sad," I said. "You still have your children—your five sons and five daughters."

51

She answered simply: "You do not yet realize, Ingrid, what it means to lose your life partner."

Now I knew. I thought back to all the difficult tasks that had occupied my last days in Germany, before my flight from Frankfurt to New York. All the legal papers had to be signed. I filled out endless German forms, made a new will, exchanged Walter's station wagon for a smaller car, and met with the steering committee of Family Life Mission. One member of the group had said: "The captain of our ship is gone. Now we on board have to get the ship safely to shore and regroup." An experienced mission leader and friend spoke to me openly when we talked about the future of FLM: "Be ready to go through many crises." And in my new grief I was still so sensitive and subjective. Even decisions that I knew were right could hurt me deeply.

I thought back to the first Christmas without Walter. In spite of the joy of Daniel and Betty's wedding and the pleasure of being together, I couldn't get over the feeling that our family, too, was shipwrecked. Our tight little family boat had capsized. We were all bobbing around in the water. But we did have our life belts on. No one was drowning, and yet we were conscious of the danger. All three of my sons had been in freak accidents that could have killed them, but they were left with only scars.

The Norwegian painter Monch has depicted the death of his sister in the painting, "Chamber of Death." All the family members are in the room, but they look in different directions—isolated from one another. Each is reacting in an individual way to the tragedy.

My grief as a bereaved wife was not the same grief as

that of my children, who had lost their father. This in turn made me feel separated, not only from Walter, but also from my sons and daughters. Each one of us was dealing with grief in our own way. Would we ever find our orientation again? I could understand better, now, what Paul wrote to the Romans: "The whole creation groans in bondage" (Rom 8:22). My heart still groans. Sometimes it seems like nothing but a ball of pain. But I am comforted through it all with little glimpses of light through the clouds. A Jewish rabbi once said, "There is nothing more whole than a broken heart."

As my plane approached New York, I felt that ball of pain again. I remembered the last time I had traveled a long distance by myself, to Port Moresby, in Papua New Guinea. There was Walter waiting with open arms to greet me. He had lovingly prepared every detail for my arrival. Never again would that happen. I remembered what Nouwen had said in *The Wounded Healer*: "No man can stay alive when nobody is waiting for him. Everyone who returns from a long and difficult trip is looking for someone waiting for him at the station or the airport."

Walter's memorial service in Minneapolis was held on January 20. Dr. William Berg, the pastor who had introduced us when we were both students at Augustana College, was in charge of the Sunday afternoon service. Our Ethiopian friend, Getahun, wearing the traditional festive white garments of his country, gave the message. As he stood in the pulpit, raising his hands in praise and lifting up his eyes, he said, "Let's be silent and celebrate Walter's wedding with the heavenly bridegroom." Then he read the text from Joshua 1:1-9: "Moses, my servant, is dead. . . . Arise, cross the Jordan, and possess the land." A youth choir sang anthems of praise. Many of these young people had heard Walter speak at the Lutheran Youth Encounter Convention in Minneapolis just a few months earlier.

My brother sang, and one of my sisters gave her tribute. My daughter Katrine honored her father with one sentence: "He never put me down."

All I could say was, "The man and his message were one. Walter practiced what he preached." I shared what Becky Pippert, a special friend, had written, "Shining brightly, Walter left us. His trip to the States in the fall was like that last burst of sunlight before the sun went down."

Not until this celebration service did it become clear to me how my own brothers and sisters had looked to Walter as a brother—even as a father. As Carl, a younger brother, put it, "There was no one like this brother—no one like him as a pastor." I felt the pain of my nieces and nephews, whom Walter had loved and with whom he had developed a special relationship. Would I be able to help them—spurring them on to combat darkness with light?

Before returning to Europe, I spent three days in the home of a close friend. She asked questions and listened as I talked. It was the first time I could put much of my grief into words. Since her husband was away on a business trip, we were alone in their uncluttered home. The atmosphere of loving care, together with the hot tea graciously served, helped me to share what I had not been able to before. At the end of the third day, I felt a great lump pass from my throat—a symbol of all the inner pain that had been in my heart.

To be alone—and yet not lonely? To accept my condition with its limitations? Life has no guarantees, and I can take none of God's gifts for granted. Once more, I pondered the words of Amy Carmichael: "In acceptance lieth peace." I was intensely lonely, not only because I had lost my life's partner, but because I was watching each one of my children move into worlds of their own. How would I make peace with it? Where now was my world?

I picked up Elisabeth Elliot's book, *These Strange Ashes,* and read: "It was a long time before I came to the realization that it is in our acceptance of what is given that God gives Himself. Even the Son of God had to learn obedience by the things which He suffered. . . . Amy Carmichael wrote:

But these strange ashes, Lord, this nothingness.
This baffling sense of loss?
Son, was the anguish of my stripping less
    Upon the torturing cross?

We may learn to accept each separate experience of individual stripping as a fragment of what the suffering Christ bore on the cross. 'Surely He hath borne our griefs and carried our sorrows.' I may accept this grief, this sorrow, this total loss that empties my hands and breaks my heart. And by accepting it, I find in my hands something to offer. And so I give it back to him, who in mysterious exchange gives himself to me."

"Then your gloom shall be like the midday" or, as another translation has it, "Your darkness will be as bright as noon" (Is 58:10). This was the promise in my heart as I left New York for Frankfurt, Germany. My friend and editor in New York, Ed Sammis, had told me of his experience with grief, "When you hear the first bird singing, then you know that you are at the end of the tunnel."

Stephen met me in Frankfurt. It was only the first week in February, but I did hear a bird singing outside my window the next morning. I also heard the news that the FLM Steering Committee was working toward incorporation. This little tree, Family Life Mission, was growing and spreading its branches.

As for my part, I could only "take the next indicated step," as my brother Carl advised me. Our first FLM marriage seminar was scheduled to be given in Salzburg a few weeks later. The three couples in charge asked me to be a part of the team. I accepted with fear and trembling, knowing how much it would hurt to do something for the first time that Walter and I had always done together. Yet I knew it was a step I should take.

February 17—my first birthday since Walter's death. The year before we had celebrated together, and our circle was complete. The watchword for the day had been from Psalm 102:17: "He will listen to the prayer of the destitute [of those stripped of everything]." I had not understood it then, for it seemed as if my cup was running over and my hands were full. This year the watchword from the *Moravian Daily Texts* was Isaiah

55:8: "For my thoughts are not your thoughts, neither are your ways my ways, says the Lord. For as the heavens are higher than the earth, so are my ways higher than your ways and my thoughts than your thoughts."

After our FLM seminar in Salzburg, where we experienced great blessings, I took time out at a quiet place for a week of renewal. I was deeply grateful for this chance to get a new perspective on the months ahead. I had read that a widow should make no major decisions in her life for at least a year—but I needed to know which direction God was leading me.

In my journal, I wrote down these priorities:

1. To be an obedient daughter to my heavenly Father—
   (a) to read his word and listen to his voice daily
   (b) to take time for worship and prayer (for me that also means time to crawl up on my heavenly Father's lap and let myself be loved). God respects us when we work for him, but he loves us when we sing to him. Teach me, Father, to sing again.
2. To be the mother of my children no matter how many miles separate us. They are always in my heart, and this includes my children-in-love and my precious grandchildren.
3. To be a nurturing mother to the growth of Family Life Mission in Germany, Africa, Austria, France, and the United States. This means continuing the three-fold ministry which Walter and I had developed together and encouraging our co-workers in the same:
   (a) conducting Family Life Seminars
   (b) writing projects—get Walter's unfinished

manuscript on the "Man" ready for publication.

(c) answering letters from readers of our books who asked for counsel in their family problems. We need a network of friends who speak the major world languages to help in this quiet ministry.

4. To be a "place" for those who need it. To nurture the prophets, especially dedicated youth who are in search of their life ministry. This means to replan and make order in our tiny home on the Lichtenberg—to consolidate the old and be wide open for the new.

If Walter was a "morning" person, perhaps I am an "evening" person. My favorite time of the day is that golden hour just before and after the sun sets. "Lord, help me to use these golden hours. The doors to the whole world are open."

On the Saturday before Easter, "Silent Saturday" they call it in Germany, I went to the cemetery in Attersee. Pastor Fuchs, who married us and counseled us over the years, always advised us on this day to place in the grave all our resentments and our bitterness against those who may have wronged us. We were to take all our self-pity and leave it there.

I went to Walter's grave and placed on it the burdens which were still with me. My heart was sore, like a child crying for comfort. I had not yet grown up as far as my grief went. As I dealt with one layer of it, yet another layer would be exposed and the "grief work" continued, like peeling the layers off an onion. As I stood at Walter's grave the sun broke through the clouds and I sensed my risen Lord. The words I heard were simply: "Except a grain of wheat fall into the ground and die, it abides by itself alone. But if it dies, it bears much fruit."

Many little trees were growing up from Walter's careful and caring counseling ministry. My task, now, was to be a gardener, to strengthen those that were weak, to cultivate, to cut and prune, and also to await the right time, God's time. I wanted to be like Isaiah 61:3: "A tree of righteousness—a planting to His praise."

Easter Sunday came and Betty, my daughter-in-love, wrote to me:

May our Good Shepherd lead you
   beside still waters,
      pools of deep rest
        and restore your life
greening the dark expanse of a grieving soul
   caring and carrying you for His name's sake.

Contrary to the general assumption, the first days of grief are not the worst. The immediate reaction is usually shock and numbing disbelief. One has undergone an amputation. After shock comes acute early grief. . . . One still feels the lost limb down to the nerve endings. It is as if the intensity of grief fused the distance between you and the dead. Or, perhaps, in reality, part of one dies. Like Orpheus, one tries to follow the dead on the beginning of their journey. But one cannot, like Orpheus, go all the way, and after a long journey one comes back. If one is lucky, one is reborn. Some people die and are reborn many times in their lives. For others the ground is too barren and the time too short for rebirth. Part of the process is the growth of a new relationship with the dead, that "veritable ami mort" Saint Exupery speaks of. Like all gestation, it is a slow, dark, wordless process. While it is taking place, one is painfully vulnerable. One must guard and protect the new life growing within—like a child.

Anne Lindbergh
Hour of Gold, Hour of Lead

Our little house is in the front center, surrounded by four farmers' homes.

SEVEN

The Stages of Grief

A FTER ALL THE ACTIVITIES AND TRAVEL necessary in those first months following Walter's death, I wanted to spend a quiet summer with the children on the Lichtenberg. Ruth had just graduated from high school in Salzburg. She offered to take care of the cooking.

Walter's best friend, Wolfgang Caffier, now a retired pastor in Dresden, was to be our guest for six weeks. We would work together on Walter's last manuscript and on his journals.

With a twinkle in his eyes, Walter had often said, "My wife wrote a book entitled *The Joy of Being a Woman*. I'm going to write one about *The Pain of Being a Man*." The first handwritten draft of the book lay on his desk when he died. Also in his office was a box which his mother had carefully packed and arranged. It contained his journals and the letters he had written to her as a young man. They were all in German script.

"Someday I will read them to you," he had told me, but that "someday" had never come. I knew that Wolfgang could decipher them for me.

As I opened my mail, there was a letter from one of my

best friends, Helen Fagerberg. Her husband had died suddenly, in much the same way as Walter. He was one of the great Bible teachers of our generation and had served for many years as Dean of the Lutheran Bible Institute in Minneapolis. Three weeks after his death, as she went back to his office to clear out his papers and books, she met one of his fellow teachers. He greeted her in the empty hallway and asked her, "You're all right now, aren't you, Helen?" "No, I'm not all right," she answered. A helpless silence followed.

When she told me of this experience, I thought of the study done by a journalist after the Vietnam War. He asked people, "How long is it normal to mourn the loss of a loved one?" The overwhelming majority thought that individuals should be done with mourning between forty-eight hours and two weeks after a death!

To swallow grief may make a person sick. Helen told me later, as we discussed the stages of grief and their expression, "Sometimes I feel sad for me because of the great sadness I feel."

As for me, I knew that I, too, was not "all right." "I haven't lost Walter," I thought, "because I know where he is. I've lost myself! I no longer have an identity as the wife of Walter Trobisch, not even as the mother of his children. Who am I?" A friend urged me to accept my loneliness, to be at home in my own heart, to discover the center of life there. I couldn't yet grasp it.

Anne Lindbergh's book, *Hour of Gold, Hour of Lead,* shares her thoughts after the kidnapping and death of her first child: "Grief is a great leveler. There is no high road out. Courage is the first step, but simply to bear the blow bravely is not enough. Stoicism is courageous, but it is only a halfway house on the long road. It is a shield, permissible for a short time only. In the end, one has to discard shields and remain vulnerable. Otherwise, scar tissues will seal off the wound and no growth will follow. To grow, to be reborn, one must remain vulnerable— open to love, but also hideously open to the possibility of more suffering."

I had indeed been putting on a brave front. "Don't be ashamed to admit your own needs, Mother," my oldest son told me. Why did I mourn for that which was past? Was the pain I felt after Walter's death greater than that which I had felt before, when I was so acutely aware of my separation from him during his trips away from home or when he was so completely absorbed in a manuscript or involved in counseling others?

Again, I was drawn to the words of Anne Lindbergh after the death of her little son: "I do not believe that sheer suffering teaches. If suffering alone taught, all the world would be wise, since everyone suffers. To suffering must be added mourning, understanding, patience, love, openness, and the willingness to remain vulnerable."

In my journal entry of August 1, 1980, I wrote: "May I have the willingness in my mourning to remain vulnerable." I had found in Walter's office a little blue, cloth-bound journal which was still full of empty pages. It had been a special gift to him from his oldest daughter. I felt an inner need to write to Walter on those pages, sharing my deepest feelings. Every afternoon I would steal away from our little beehive of a house and sit on the lonely bench, where we had so often sat together drinking in the beauty of the Alpine foothills. And there I would write.

August 1, 1980

My dear departed,

I found this book in your office. I'm going to use it these next days and weeks to write to you. I feel the need of making peace with my memories, the joyful ones, but also the hurting ones.

When I was visiting your cousin in East Germany last month, I had a dream that I was driving your station wagon. Remember the one our children called "Maxi"? I had to go to the airport to catch a flight. As I drove out of the driveway, the car plunged straight down into a deep pit. There was no stopping my going down, down, until the car caught on the side of the abyss and I was saved.

There are times when I am not courageous or "noble." (Someone told me once, "Don't try to be noble. Just be real.") Sometimes I want to cry bitterly. Mostly it's a weeping for that which eluded me in our marriage, for all those times when I felt myself going down into a pit. There were also times when you reached out your hand, just in time to save me from going all the way down. I remember those sleepless nights, with you sleeping soundly at my side. Daniel would ask me at breakfast how I had slept. My answer: "Very poorly." He would ask, "Mother, what's your conflict?"

Maybe that's why I have to write to you now, as the late afternoon sun is casting its golden rays on the mountains surrounding us, in order to resolve some of the conflicts which I still feel when I think of you.

One of our conflicts was *time*. You seemed to be always ahead of yourself. I was always a little behind, panting to keep up with your giant strides, and feeling like I never quite made it. How often I wanted simply to enjoy the "sacrament of the present moment," after we had finished a project. But you were already making plans for the next. One of your favorite phrases was, *Es hat geklappt* (See, how nicely it all worked out). And then you would go to sleep the moment your head touched the pillow. I was left behind. Even Sunday afternoons, after we had coffee, you would often say that you had to dictate letters, or that some young person wanted to have a talk with you.

As I sit quietly on my bench and read what I have written to you, I heard your answer:

August 3

But, Ingrid, I've heard all that before. Aren't you happy that you had a husband who knew how to use his time? Time must be structured if it is to have value. I tried to be "on target" or "on track" and do that which I felt guided to do, that which we decided together had to be done. You were not fair.

Didn't I tell you over and over that in every line I wrote, every talk I gave, every letter I wrote—you were with me? Men are different than women. What makes them completely satisfied, fulfilled, at peace, can be for their wives just the beginning. This is true both in his work, for if a man likes his work, he likes himself, and in his experience of sexual love.

Often I could see the hurt look on your face. There was that little girl in you who always needed comfort. I needed your understanding. You wanted sometimes to be one of my "counselees," and I didn't like that. I wanted a happy, cheerful, uncomplicated wife. Why was this so difficult for you? Why do you remember only the hard times and forget the good times? Can you recall all those times when heaven came to someone through being in our home? All those celebrations we had as a family, the confirmations and birthday parties for our children, those fifteen wonderful Christmases at the Lichtenberg. Do you think the devil knows how to celebrate?

Don't you understand that even now when I have left you for my heavenly home, that you can use our "earthly tent" to God's glory, as a place where you and our children can find peace and be strengthened? Not only you, but many others. Our little home was one of the most precious gifts of our marriage, and God is not done with it yet.

August 7

Liebes!

Today your brother came for a visit. In him, I saw you again. I gave him the photo albums that your parents had so lovingly put together of all your family trips.

Then I asked Klaus why your letters as a young man were only addressed to your mother. He said that it was always easier for you to talk to your mother and that you and your father often did not see eye-to-eye. You could also be very critical of your father and told him how you felt. I noticed that you did not have many close men friends—there were few who seemed to be up to your standards. You could also be very untactful and wounding with some of our best friends. I think back to the last week of your life—how you were hurt by your own sons as they loosened the cords binding them to the "father" pole . . ."

August 8

Ingrid, my faithful one who stood true to me through thick and thin! It is true—I did have a special relationship with my mother, and we were much alike. Because of her, I learned to respect women and was not threatened by them. I felt that my mother had a deeper insight into problems and even politics than did my good father. Yes, I was sometimes sharp and critical of other men. If I could not tell you of my hostile feelings, to whom could I talk? I didn't want you to rise to their defense. I needed your ears and I needed to hear you say, "Walter, I understand. That is how you feel." Remember, feelings are neither right nor wrong. They just are.

Don't forget that I was called to be a Nathan for many of these men. When it came to sin, I could only help them by shocking them out of their lethargy and rationalization. Sometimes they ran away. At other times, after struggling through to obedience to God's word, they came back. I had to be strong for my own sons, too, like the pole to which the small tree is tied. Only then can the little tree grow strong and straight and not be broken off by the first winds that come along. Think of all our African sons—Emmanuel, Jean, Justin, Pierre, Joseph, and many others—who are being faithful witnesses in their countries.

Didn't I become "mellow" and learn better how to express my deep feelings in those last years, months, weeks? But my time on earth is finished. You go and do better with your mildness. Don't forget that sometimes you must use the pruning hook too.

Dein Walter

August 9

Liebes!

Today Wolfgang gave me the letter you wrote to your mother and the poems that were her Christmas present in 1942. You were just nineteen and an infantry soldier on the Russian front. All around you was the threat of death. Those little pieces of pencil-written paper in your pocket kept you alive. You had to send them to your mother, and in order to send them you had to stay alive.

As I read those words, I could now feel what you were feeling. At the beginning of our marriage and so many times later on, I was not able to do that. Remember how you told me laughingly as we were getting acquainted, "I am the master of my heart." I guess you had to be when you were in Germany after the war as a young unmarried pastor. There was only one man for every seven women. I respected you because I could trust you, and love is built on respect. But I couldn't always find your feelings.

Now I know the feelings were there. I felt you reaching out to me on that last evening of your life. You wondered why our friends hadn't called after our trip. "Does anyone still love me?" you asked. It was the call of the child who is hurting and wants to be comforted; it was the call of the wounded soldier; and it was the call of the mature man, longing for love and understanding.

One of your favorite verses was Isaiah 66:13: "Like a man whom his mother comforts, so will I comfort you, and you will be comforted in Jerusalem." Now you are comforted. I know, too, that it was because of your mother's happy, unconditional love and your father's careful protection and provision that you were secure and accepting of yourself. Because of their love and because of your final security in Jesus Christ, you could reach out and help others.

But I have one final question: wouldn't another wife have been better for you—the petite, dark-haired type, like your mother? Why was it so hard for me to believe that you loved me sometimes? Again I have that deep lump in my throat.

August 10

My dear partner that I had to leave behind when I went on my last great journey, because our work wasn't finished yet. Remember, Ingrid, I gave you my complete trust when I left home on my teaching and speaking trips. I told you many times how grateful I was to have a wife who was capable of making wise decisions and acting independently of me when we were separated. That's why I married you, because I couldn't imagine any other partner who would be willing to take the risks you took with me and to stand so faithfully by my side.

You're right. You were not like my mother. I did not want a second mother. I wanted a wife. But because I had such a wonderful mother, I could love you the more and not less. Look in the mirror and say, "I am a beautiful woman. I like what I see." And then go your way, forgetting everything except that others need your love. I loved you and tried to show it to you in every way I could. You couldn't always accept it, because you couldn't always accept yourself. Stop thinking less of yourself than I thought of you, than Christ thought of you. Didn't we both lay down our lives for you?

I tried to be a father—a loving father, but also a strict father—not only for those in my own family, but also for those who came to me for spiritual help. I was always sincere, even if at times I may have been naive. Forgive me for my mistakes and then forget. Remember what I always told my counselees, "To take a forgiven sin back upon your shoulders is to commit a new sin."

Now get up and take your staff and walk. The Lord has promised you: "I will send an angel before you, to guide you on the way and to bring you to the place I have prepared for you. . . . My presence shall go with you and I will give you rest."

Your husband of twenty-seven years

I continued my dialogue with Walter in the little blue journal. Sometimes I could share my thoughts with Wolfgang, who was a true "friend of the bridegroom." He gave me a helpful quotation from Raabe, a German poet, who said, "In the moment when the true artist is creating, he has neither wife nor child, and least of all, friends." This word comforted me when I thought of all those lonely times when Walter was "creating."

I had gone to the cemetery on the first anniversary of Walter's funeral and afterwards wrote the last entry in the blue journal: "It's a year ago today that we laid your earthly body reverently and thankfully to rest. I want to thank you for your life and for all you have given me, for your faithful love of thirty years, beginning when you stood in that crowded church in Rock Island, when I was being commissioned. Today I am filled with awe when I see our magnificent children (and I use the word reverently). For me you are living on in each child and grandchild.

"I went to your grave, but you were not there. I went to our bench, but found only memories. Our house was filled with golden light and with promises for the future. As I left the Lichtenberg, the heavens were breath-taking, a lovely royal purple tone was evident even in the browns of the earth. Will it be like this when Jesus returns to the earth?"

It is hard to believe that Father left us already a year ago. He is more alive and closer to me than ever in my mind and spirit. He will always be to me a great light shining from the distance and showing the way. He will also be a symbol for the "unfulfilled desires" of which he so often talked—in that he himself has become unreachable in a physical way—pointing to another source from which all our needs can be met.

Katrine Trobisch Stewart
New Delhi, India

With Katrine and baby Charles.

EIGHT

A Promise of Joy

AFTER KATRINE HAD WRITTEN these words to me, she
invited me to spend several weeks with her and her
family in New Delhi, India. Her husband, David Stewart,
taught at the American Embassy School. She promised
that my only responsibility would be to enjoy my two
small granddaughters, Christine and Virginia. I arranged
my schedule so that I could leave the second week in
December and stay with them for two months. The
cheapest way to travel would be on Aeroflot, the Russian
airline, in an overnight flight from Vienna, via Moscow,
to New Delhi.

Rarely can I sleep on such flights. It's that wonderful
"in-between" time, letting go of one world and experience before another begins. I thought back to the last
intensive weeks, when I had taken part in Family Life
Seminars in Germany and Austria. It was only with great
fear and trembling that I had done so. God had greatly
blessed the seeds that were sown. How often I had felt
Walter at my side, his hand on my shoulder saying, "Go
ahead. You can do it. Take that first step."

Before Wolfgang Caffier had returned to his home in

Dresden, he had conducted a little service for us at the time that Walter's gravestone had been set up permanently. He based his thoughts on Jeremiah 29:11, "I know the plans I have for you—plans for your welfare and not for evil—to give you a future and a hope." How many times had I been given that strong word of God since the death of my husband—"a future and a hope?" It was time to really let go of the past and to look to the future.

I traveled east all night, in the direction of the rising sun. As our plane landed at the Delhi International Airport just as the sun was rising, I felt a surge of joy and the promise of Proverbs 4:18 came to mind, "The path of the righteous is like the light of dawn, which shines brighter and brighter until full day."

As I passed through customs I caught sight of my auburn-haired daughter and my sturdy little granddaughters, Christine, three and a half, and Virginia, eighteen months, waving their welcome. These are my future and my hope, I thought. How thankful I am that David and Katrine believe in parenthood when so many of their peers have opted for childlessness. I certainly agreed with a friend who said that becoming a grandparent was the only stage of life with which there was nothing wrong. Walter had experienced that joy, too, before he left us. He had held and blessed his two granddaughters during our last days together in the States.

As Katrine and I sat hand in hand, the two little ones snuggled on our laps, we knew the glad joy of reunion. Our old but elegant black taxi was skillfully maneuvered through traffic by a Sikh driver. My tired eyes were overwhelmed by color—the dark greens of the foliage contrasted beautifully with the flamboyant orange-red flowers and delicate lavender blossoms. Even the earth tones and rocks seemed alive. I felt as if I had been lifted out of a black-and-white world—the dull gray of Vienna in December—into a world filled with color and sunshine.

Katrine and David had a large apartment in the embassy school compound, and their guest room had been lovingly prepared. A beautiful bouquet of red roses stood on the little desk, and there was even a rocking chair. I already felt at home.

After being greeted warmly by my son-in-law during his class break, I sank into a deep sleep. Jet lag had caught up with me. As I awoke, I recalled my dream. I was holding a baby in my arms. The baby called repeatedly for Walter. A large conference was ready to begin with many rooms full of people. I knew some of the people and asked them to help me find my husband. I called, but Walter didn't come. He's probably counseling someone and cannot be disturbed, I thought.

Later, when I told Katrine and David about the dream, I realized that the little baby I was holding represented the infant stage of Family Life Mission. Could it survive without Walter?

One sign of life is growth. Was I growing? In the sheltered family atmosphere of my daughter's home, I was removed from all the stress of the last months. I had become very lazy. After a few days, even writing a postcard seemed a difficult task. An embassy nurse remarked that a certain amount of stress is healthy, but that there are times, too, when we need "to give our roots rain."

Reading was one of the ways I could do this. For the first time, I read the biography of Eleanor Roosevelt. She told one of her aides: "Don't forget to tell your wife every day that she is your number one person. So many husbands take this for granted." As I pondered this thought, I realized that I had no one anymore for whom I was number one. I shared my pain with Katrine. She wisely reminded me that I must again revert to the time of adolescence and learn anew the secret of living with unfulfilled desires.

We talked about remorse in the grief process, that remorse is just as dangerous and as much of a dead end as self-pity. It's like beating oneself to make what *has* happened "unhappen." Anne Lindbergh calls it "fooling yourself, feeding on an illusion; just as living on memories, clinging to relics and photographs, is an illusion. Like the food offered in dreams, it will not nourish; no growth or rebirth will come from it."

As we sat on the park bench, watching Christine and Virginia play, I shared with Katrine what her father had written in his marriage dialog notebook. We had agreed to write down the answer to the question: "If someone wants to understand me in depth, what are the ten most important things he has to know about me?"

This is what Walter had written, just before we had left on our last journey together.

1. That I have been ready to die many times; therefore everything in the here and now is secondary—even inconsequential—in light of the hope of eternal life.

2. That basically I am not a go-getter, fighter, or invader, but rather a withdrawn spectator, a quiet enjoyer of life, who feels uncomfortable in the lime-light.

3. That I depend ultimately on God and that I can face, endure, and enjoy life only because I am *not* dependent on it.

4. That I live in constant fear of being overpowered by an anonymous, demonic force of organization, admin-istration, bureaucracy, be it of church or state. I love and need freedom.

5. That my wife and children mean more to me than any other human beings, and that my relationship to them is secondary only to my relationship to Jesus Christ.

6. That I am happiest when I am creative and that for this, voluntarily chosen and granted solitude is at times more precious and important to me than fellow-ship.

7. That I enjoy helping others both inwardly and outwardly.

8. That sexuality is for me one aspect of enjoyment among others; one expression of love among others, but not basic.

9. That I love shelteredness, comfortableness, having an overview, order, and a regular schedule. That I have a far greater longing to explore the inner world than the wide outer world. The paradox is that the more I succeed in reaching the depths of the inner world (books!), the more the burden of the outer world becomes my own.

10. That I only lose perspective of things when I do not have enough sleep, and that I cannot find sleep when I lose perspective (a vicious circle).

Walter and I had begun our marriage dialog notebooks while attending our first Marriage Encounter weekend in Minneapolis. We had just taught six Family Life Seminars together in New Guinea, Australia, and the States and were in desperate need for renewal ourselves. The first question we were told to answer, each one in our separate notebooks, was, "Why did you come to this weekend?" I quickly wrote down as my first point: "In order to find help in our marriage." Walter's first point was: "In order to learn new things to help others in their marriage."

Another question we had to answer was: "What was the happiest time in your marriage up till now?" I remember how surprised I was at Walter's answer: "Translating your book, *The Joy of Being a Woman,* into German." At the time, I was in the hospital recuperating from a kidney operation. Each morning, he would work on the translation, and in the afternoon he would read his handwritten pages to me when he came to visit. It was a true labor of love. For him, blank sheets of paper and undisturbed time contained the essence of happiness.

Walter could say a lot, even on a postcard. I found one in my papers which he had written to me from Heidelberg years earlier when he was working on his doctoral studies. He stayed with his mother in Mannheim, while I was with the children on the Lichtenberg. He told me how he had been able to help a young nurse in her decision to let go of an old relationship and begin a new one with Jesus Christ. He wrote: "There were two things in this case which comfort me deeply: (1) Our wonderful cooperation and oneness in spirit to help her as a counseling team. Without your two letters to her, the operation could not have been performed in such a short time. (2) A new certainty about my message combining soul care and private confession, which for me goes hand in hand with marriage counseling. Here is the forgotten key and the only explanation for the fifty-six translations of *I Loved a Girl.* I have no bad conscience about this waste of time, as one of our pastors called it. God will give time for the ministry to which he has called us."

That was in 1965. The young nurse whom Walter had helped later assisted me in nursing my mother-in-law through her terminal illness at the Lichtenberg.

In my journal, I had pasted the note he had written to me on June 2, 1979, our last wedding anniversary.

My dear Ingrid, you are that which is most precious to me in this world and I thank you ever anew, that you have walked with me the long route of these twenty-seven years, through heights and depths, and have never given up. Above all I want to thank you for your compassion when I was weak and your patience with all my incapabilities. It would seem that we have become poorer during this last year—in both our own relationship and with our children. But in the carrying together and the acceptance of this poverty is there not also a newer, deeper dimension of our marriage?

> Pledged to you in troth,
> Your husband who loves you

It is Christmas. I spend it quietly with my daughter and her husband in the beautiful surroundings of the international quarter of New Delhi. It is a break with the tradition of Christmas on the Lichtenberg. Pastor Berg writes to me: "Walter is home for Christmas this year." In December 1942, Walter had written his parents from the foxholes outside of Stalingrad: "Nothing is greater in me than my longing for a homecoming in the Kingdom of Love."

A few months earlier, as he was leaving Poland for the Russian front, he had written in his journal: "Never before did I experience the nearness of Christ as yesterday when I walked to the railroad station. He was walking beside me, clearly and earnestly. He was in me. He walked ahead of me. Yes, he even protected me from behind."

If Christ could do it for a nineteen-year-old German soldier almost forty years ago, he could do it now for his widow.

"Ingrid, you are not to conserve the past," an Austrian friend wrote, "but keep on going toward heaven. Keep your eyes off the earth and lift them up to heaven."

Something happened to me during those quiet sabbatical weeks in New Delhi. I told Katrine and David that I had no desire to see India as a tourist, discovering the sights and smells of this magnificent land. Outside of a weekend trip with Katrine to the bird sanctuary at Bharatour, combined with a bus trip to Agra to see the Taj Mahal in all of its breathtaking beauty, I kept close to their home. The daily walks with my grandchildren opened my eyes to color as never before. I discovered the lavender hue in the early evening skies, the grey green of the eucalyptus trees blending with the deep green of the tropical foliage. I saw the exquisite taste and colors in the dress of the Indian women. My world, which had been gray for so long, was suddenly bursting with color. My daughter encouraged me to put down what I was seeing on canvas. We sketched and painted together. It was a new beginning for me and one which was to lead me down many paths of joy in the months and years to come.

In two weeks I would return to Europe. I would have a full schedule until the end of the year. Lectures and seminars were to be held in both southern and northern Germany. A trip was also planned to East Germany. In August, I would return to Africa to help our African team in two training seminars in Ghana. After that I would travel to the States.

"One must live in the present moment," Stephen, my youngest son wrote, "even when it is not to be stopped. It's good that we can't make time go either slower or faster. It is the love of God which carries us through all times, never ceasing, as the strongest power."

David and Katrine decided to invite their international friends to a Viennese House Ball. They moved the furniture out of their large living and dining room area. Garlands of flowers were draped from the walls to the center of the ceiling. Austrian food specialities were prepared by Katrine and her faithful Indian cook. The strains of Johann Strauss' "Blue Danube Waltz" filled the room. As the dancing began, I felt as though I was dreaming. *One,* two, three. *One,* two, three. David was guiding me skillfully, and I was glad that my feet still knew how to waltz.

Later one of the guests, a retired Indian officer asked me, "What is your secret?"

"I don't understand," I said, "What do you mean?"

"There is something in your face—your daughter has it too—which I have not often seen in women from the West. I would call it serenity." I took it as an affirmation. Serenity means suffering overcome.

As I prepared for my departure, I thanked my children again for this wonderful evening of celebration. "I held it in memory of my father," Katrine said. "He taught me how to plan such an evening."

"For me the evening was like a light at the end of a tunnel," I replied. "I know now that my life did not end with your father's death. Both of you and your children have given me joy and hope for the future."

If a widow can't readjust to living with herself, she certainly can't be expected to readjust to living with another person. . . .

"Marry in haste, repent at leisure" is a moral not just for young people.

Marriage is never an "escape." Rather at any age a couple should be willing to ask themselves whether they are more effective for Christ together than they are apart. . . . People wrapped up in the solving of their own problems cannot be effective in solving problems of others.

Those who live in a state of perpetual mourning do their mates no honor. Rather remarriage is the highest praise one can pay to a deceased mate. It says, in effect, "Marriage is good and I want to be a part of that good relationship again."

If a woman can leave that choice to God, trusting Him for either the single or the married life, she is truly the freest of all His creation. In complete dependence upon God, she finds that she does not need to depend on an earthly relationship for her well-being. . . .

The widow committed to God has learned through her experience that her fellowship is with One who will not get moody and out of sorts. Her Provider is One who owns the cattle on a thousand hills. Her Comforter is One who truly understands, because He has shared her infirmity. Her Beloved is none other than the great I Am.

Judith Fabisch
Not Ready to Walk Alone

This portrait was taken in Salzburg before one of our last tours.

NINE

To Marry Again?

"A PART OF YOU IS BURIED with Walter; a part of Walter lives on in you." An Austrian friend had spoken these words to me on the first anniversary of Walter's death. If this were true, and I believed it was, could I ever think of remarriage?

Dr. Theo Bovet, our own marriage counselor, had written in his last book: "The continual deepening of the marriage relationship outlives the erotical fellowship and can be especially radiant in old age. It outshines the hour of death and gives the strange certainty that marriage does not end with physical death" (*Mensch sein,* Katzman Verlag).

My oldest son, Daniel, had written to me: "Don't be ashamed of your needs, but learn to listen to them and accept them quietly. That will give you peace in listening to others. Don't be afraid of showing your needs. Age is less relevant than you think. You have a right to need."

It had taken me many years of marriage to learn that no man on this earth can satisfy the deepest needs in a woman's heart. The "little child" in my heart longed to be comforted, and I could not understand why he, who could comfort so many others, could not also be my comforter.

My father had died and was buried in a lonely grave during World War II in Dar es Salaam, East Africa. I was only sixteen at the time of his death and had been deprived of his caring presence during those precious teenage years when a daughter desperately needs her father's love and affirmation. I can't remember weeping when we received the news of his sudden death. I kept a stiff upper lip and thought my job was to comfort my mother and younger brothers and sisters. My father had always been my hero. I suppose that by not allowing myself to grieve for him, I was trying to be a hero too.

One day, over thirty years later, I was alone at the Lichtenberg. Walter had taken the children on a mountain-climbing tour. I remember watching the movie version of *A Tree Grows in Brooklyn* on television. All the floodgates in my heart broke loose as I empathized with the twelve-year-old girl weeping for her dead father. It seemed hours before I could stop crying. I realize now that this was a preparation for the loss of my husband a few years later. How, otherwise, could I have coped with a new loss, if I had not grieved for the first loss?

But now I had lost Walter, that very special person in my life. I knew that I could not heal the hurt of losing my husband by replacing him with another. First the wound had to heal. Only then would I be capable of making wise decisions for the future.

The temptation to try to replace a beloved partner is strongest in the first year after experiencing loss. How can one endure the loneliness without thoughts of someone to take the loved one's place?

I recall the letter of condolence I received from a widower. He was Walter's age, and his life as a doctor was committed to helping people. His wife had died after a long illness a few months before Walter's death. He wanted me to know that I could count on him as an understanding friend. He came to visit me one beautiful June afternoon, and we walked together through one of the loveliest parks in Europe. A month later he invited me to visit him at his well-ordered home. It was a cool, rainy afternoon, and he had built a cozy fire in the fireplace. He asked me to sit in his wife's comfortable chair and then played one of his favorite records, a violin concerto by Bach. We drank coffee together and talked freely.

I couldn't believe that this was actually happening to me, this moment of complete happiness, of having a man whom I could respect give me this feeling of being sheltered and cared for again. He had even prepared a gourmet dinner, which we enjoyed together before he brought me to the station to catch the last train home that evening.

We wrote occasionally after that. Then one day he stood unannounced on my doorstep at the Lichtenberg. I was flustered. It was not a good time for me to have visitors since I had other commitments that afternoon. I served him coffee as he sat in Walter's chair in our living room. It seemed right, and yet I picked up certain warning signals that said, "There's no future in this friendship." When I invited him to attend an international conference, he declined with the words, "I have no desire for that. I just want to bury myself in my own four walls."

Some months later, after a few telephone calls and sparse notes, he wrote that he felt incapable of involving himself in a relationship. Then he withdrew into his hermitage existence. It hurt, for I had begun to care about him. I knew that he felt something for me, but he was using enormous energy to keep his feelings buried so that he wouldn't be bothered by them. "The powerlessness to love is like the state of hell," declared a German Christian.

I learned from this experience the beauties as well as the pitfalls of friendship. How good it was to be seen again by a man. "A man falls in love with what he sees; a woman with what she hears." I learned, too, that love must be balanced. A wise Swiss woman once said: "The one who gives less love in a relationship is like a thief. The one who gives more love is like a murderer. Why? Because in the first case, one can bleed to death; in the second case, one can be strangled to death." There is the danger of being caught in a whirlpool which sucks you down and gets you nowhere. That which should come, doesn't come. It is the helpless position of being the one who gives the greater love. One is unprotected and vulnerable, until a new strength is born, the strength to love and to be vulnerable. It is the strength "to be" and not simply "to need."

When Walter died, I felt I would never want to love a man again, because I couldn't stand the pain of losing him. It was so much more comfortable to lock up my feelings and not risk being hurt. But then I learned that we don't honor the dead by dying with them. We honor them by being God's servants and stewards, by living for him and for others.

Somehow, after this experience of an aborted friendship, I could go on to the next step, wiser, more perceptive. I found special comfort in discovering in a copy of the German edition of Walter's last book, *Living with Unfulfilled Desires,* this handwritten inscription: "For my wife, who has mastered the art, better than anyone I know, of living a fulfilled life in spite of many unfulfilled wishes."

I thought of one of the couples I had talked with at a recent German seminar. He was pastor of a large parish. After a marriage of twenty-five years, he had lost his first wife unexpectedly. At her funeral he had seemed very stoical. Because he showed no outward signs of grief, his children felt separated from him. Before the year was over, he had remarried. His friends breathed a sigh of relief. Now he would be cared for and all would be fine.

But all was not fine. After three years of marriage, he and his second wife attended one of our seminars. During the course of the week, they were to answer and share with each other the questions: "What unites us the most?" "What separates us the most?" The wife was very frank when she told her husband that she felt a barrier of separation because he had never been able to share with her his grief at losing his first wife. As we talked together, the miracle happened. He was able to uncover the pain in his heart. This strong man, who was a leader for so many, was able to get in touch with his feelings again. It was as if a boil had been lanced and the pus spurted out. Then came the time of cleansing and binding up the wound which could now heal.

Losing one's partner through death or divorce means a sudden cutoff, not only of the spoken dialog, but also of the physical relationship. For the Christian, it is a time of necessary sexual fasting. True sexual intimacy involves the whole person: physically, emotionally, and spiritually. A cheap physical experience without the emotional and spiritual content will never satisfy. Our gift of sexuality is given to us as a wonderful means of communicating with one another. It is not to be turned in upon ourselves. It is possible to live without sexual activity, but it is not possible to live without affection.

Nor is it possible to live without the affirmation of others. Mark Twain said that he could live on an honest compliment for two months. I remember how my heart was warmed when after a seminar close to the borders of East Germany, a young engineer from Berlin and his wife came up to thank me for my contribution. The husband gave me a warm hug and said: "You are now a woman who belongs to all of us, Ingrid."

One widow who was asked if she would consider remarriage laughingly replied, "I have neither time in my busy schedule nor space in my crowded closet for a man." But later on, she did remarry. Certainly remarriage in God's time and with his choice is a great testimony to the institution of marriage. But what God desires, he must also inspire. He gives only the best to those who leave the choice with him. It is wrong to push open a door that God has closed.

What do people say about a person: "She's her own worst enemy" or "She's at peace with herself"? To be at peace with myself means to discover anew my five senses:

My skin—the greatest organ in the human body. My sense of touch—the feel of the wind and the rain on the skin. Swimming at least once a week, being completely surrounded by water, being carried by it, even caressed by it.

My eyes—how awesome it is when God opens our eyes "to see again." We see, not only the beauties of nature, but the greatest miracle of all, a new baby. We look at the glory of youth, splendid young adulthood, and the mature beauty of age. Yes, even wrinkles can be beautiful, for they are the shorthand of our lives.

When my eyes were opened during those weeks in India, I was hungry to see the great paintings of the world and then to learn to paint myself. It's a cleansing, happy experience to mix colors and try to capture on canvas what I see.

And the sense of taste? I feel sorry for people who eat only in order to live and work. They are missing one of the joys of life. I know a widow who caught herself one day eating her dinner out of the frying pan. If it's too much to set the table for ourselves, we can always set a tray with our best dishes, a flower, the right napkin. It's great to invite friends to share our meals. We don't have to wait to be invited. We can do the entertaining ourselves, for we will never feel like an outsider in our own home.

Our hearing? What do we feed our ears: the noisy beats of modern music or the great hymns, spirituals, classical music, and requiems? When my son Stephen visited me last year, he complained that he found only requiems in my music collection. It was true. I had listened to them over and over and had found healing for my soul. But now it was time for more joyful music.

What about our sense of smell? I love the delicate fragrance of peonies, the down-to-earth smell of baked apples, a breast-fed baby, clean linens, fresh coffee.

Even so, in spite of all these things, there is still that empty hole in my life. If I could only feel the rough tweed of Walter's jacket again. Smell his aftershave lotion, his good clean body. Have his fine, sensitive hand hold my hand. Hear his jokes and merry laughter. See his wonderful profile and high forehead.

It's easy to say, "Jesus is your husband, Ingrid." But the hole is still there. Somehow my Lord is the One who enables me to live with that hole. He hasn't filled it up yet, but he has made a bridge over it. I can live with it now, and I can stand on this bridge as I reach out to others.

Anne Lindbergh expressed this thought best in her poem *Second Sowing*, written a decade after her first child was kidnapped and killed:

For whom
The milk ungiven in the breast
When the child is gone?

For whom
The love locked up in my heart

That is left alone?
That golden yield
Split sod once, overflowed an August field,

Threshed out in pain upon September's floor.
Now hoarded high in barns, a sterile store.

Break down the bolted door;
Rip open, spread and pour
The grain upon the barren ground
Wherever crack in clod is found.

There is no harvest for the heart alone;
The seed of love must be
Eternally
Resown.

One becomes a person only if one really has a place . . . and that place is no abstraction. It is . . . the fireside, the photographs on the mantel piece, . . . the books on the shelves and all the little details with which one has become familiar. . . . Perhaps the relationship of people with places is more stable than that with their fellow human beings.

Paul Tournier
A Place for You

I'm at home again in Springfield, at *Geborgenheit*, my place of shelter.

TEN

A Place for You

I HAVE AN OLD COPPER-STUDDED TRUNK in which I packed my belongings when I left New York for Paris on my twenty-third birthday. It still has the label of the S.S. America on it. The trunk had its place in an elegant Louis XV bedroom in the Latin Quarter of Paris, where I stayed with a women doctor while earning my French teaching certificate.

My next home was in the African bush, and the trunk went with me. It became my hearth—a safe place for my photo albums, my journals, my wedding dress. Yet it was very practical. I put bricks under it, sewed a cover for it, and used it as a bathing table for our first baby.

After twelve years in Africa there came a major upheaval. We were going back to Europe. The trunk was used to encase all that which was most precious—a few of the wedding gifts that had survived, our guest book, our wooden bread plate, an African chief's carved wooden stool, books and papers that had survived the ravages of termites.

Our next home was a small prefabricated house, put up in record time in a hamlet in the Austrian mountains. We were a family seeking refuge, trying to make a "place" in the Europe of today. In an anti-child world, our family of five children was considered out of step. Our farmer neighbors warned us that our little home could not weather the winter blasts—it would surely blow away. It didn't. It housed us and kept us safe.

"It was a house in the world, and the world was in the house," as Manfred Hausman said when describing a home. The trunk was always useful, whether it was for storing blankets or sewing materials, or for protecting the treasures of a teenaged daughter.

But the dream of that home was shattered. Walter died and it seemed that our family was shipwrecked. Now its members were scattered across the world.

It was then that I decided to return to the land of my childhood, the Ozarks. No matter how much we traveled or how long we lived in foreign countries, my desire to return home to my native land only grew stronger. Somehow, an instinct deeper than reason was at work.

It had not been an easy decision. As I shared my feelings with my oldest daughter, she wrote: "I just couldn't help but feel a little 'deserted.' You're thinking of building a nest on territory that is in many ways as old as it will be new to you. . . . I would rather see you attached to people (more specifically 'family') than to a place."

My reply: "Thirty years ago I would have agreed. People are more important than places. All I wanted then was to walk at Walter's side, to be sheltered in his arms, and then I could give shelter to you, my children, and others. Now I am learning to live in peace with myself. For that I need a *place*. Only the one who has a place can be a place for others. I'm happy that Lichtenberg was your place—as it was for so many others."

It was a hard decision—to leave the old and begin anew. I claimed Psalm 73:23-24. "Nevertheless, I am continually with Thee: Thou doest hold my right hand. Thou dost guide me with Thy counsel."

One morning in July, as I awoke to a beautiful sunrise over the mountains surrounding the Lichtenberg and saw that the fog had receded to the valleys, I had a quiet, inner assurance that my heavenly Father was leading me back to Springfield and that he would show me the way, step by step.

For the first time, I shared my thoughts with my brothers and sisters. I told them about my desire to buy the old Crighton home that bordered on our childhood home. Mrs. Crighton had been our grade school teacher. Now, for health reasons, she and her husband had to sell their home of thirty-seven years. His parents had built the Ozarkian farmhouse for their large family in 1919. Yes, it was an old house, as my friends reminded me, but it radiated character and the feeling of home. My brother John wrote, "What fond memories I have of the old Crighton home! May those sturdy old stone walls now house a home which will be a blessing and a beacon of faith to coming generations."

Nigerians say that a piece of land never belongs to one person alone, but to a vast family, many of whom are dead, a few of whom are living, and a countless number of whom are unborn. I think especially of my grandchildren as I look for my place of shelter, *Geborgenheit*, so that I can give them shelter.

The way was clear, even if I didn't know just how it would be possible—especially when I thought of the financial aspect. I could sense that my time in Europe was coming to an end, that something new was being prepared. But first I, too, had to go through a birth process. I felt like a seed placed in the earth, ready to burst through, or a bud where all the explosive powers were still tightly enclosed. Everything that had to do with European bureaucracy and legal papers was strangling me. Why was everything so complicated in Europe? I had the feeling that I was constantly being forced inside a too-tight box with the lid closed down on me. I suppose that is how babies feel at the hour of birth.

I had talked over the decision with a close friend, a family therapist in Zurich. As we said goodbye, she commented: "You're different than I have ever seen you, Ingrid. It's as if something is bubbling within you out of a new source. You are no longer only Walter's wife or the mother of his children, but a person in your own right. It's all right if you go back to Missouri, but do it gradually. Don't burn your bridges behind you—you belong in both worlds. However, don't expect your children to put down their roots in Springfield."

My youngest daughter had just turned twenty, so that all my children were now in their third decade of life. I recalled the time when for a short period they had all been teenagers. It's a comfort to know that after the age of protest comes the age of change.

"I hope you can start this new part of your life with fresh strength." Ruth wrote. "Be reassured: it is the right way. Leave the old burdens behind and enjoy the new beginning. I'm sure many women will envy your decision to establish a new "place." I am proud of my mother, her example and discipleship.

"I like you more every time I see you—especially your new self-confidence." (I wonder if young people know how their parents long for a word of affirmation or even thanks from their children.)

Once more I pack my old copper-studded trunk—this time sending it from Salzburg, Austria, to Springfield, Missouri. In it are the candlesticks that have symbolized our home, a few vases and pictures, the quilt my grandmother made for me, and my special books.

"That which you have begun in faith and courage, God will help you fulfill." I wrote this in my journal as I left Frankfurt for Washington, D.C. Our DC-10 soared above the clouds where all was light. "At last I feel a firm sense of my identity. I am a child of God, a daughter of the King. A widow who mourns a beloved partner.

"My heart echoes what John Steinbeck had written to the widow of his publisher: 'I know that one seems cut off and alone before one picks up a thread and draws in a string and then a rope leading back to life again. . . . The effectiveness of a man's life can be measured by the depths of the wounds his death leaves on others.'

"I am a mother, a grandmother, a daughter, a sister to brothers and sisters, an aunt to nephews and nieces. I have a joyful ministry of speaking, teaching, and writing. Painting has become an enjoyable pastime, as well as swimming and walking. I enjoy making a 'nest,' being a hostess to others and myself. I like to nurture the prophets, especially the young ones that have not yet been recognized. I'm learning to be honest in expressing my opinion and not to withdraw from, but to resolve, conflicts.

"I'm not a mountain person, nor a sea person, but I love the trees, the rocks, and the old hills, to say nothing of the springs and caves which abound in the Ozarks."

My plane landed in Washington, D.C. "I enjoy challenges," Katrine told me after a bout with rush-hour traffic to pick me up at Washington National Airport. She and her family were in Washington preparing to leave for their new assignment in Bucharest. Six-week-old James was jostled in the baby sling around her neck and shoulders. Christine and Virginia pushed the stroller, neatly provided to carry my suitcase. I am proud of my daughter's courage and all the young mothers like her who believe in nurturing life instead of denying it. What harmony surrounds all that she and her husband do. I slept as a child myself during the nights in their home.

Since Katrine and David soon would be leaving for their new post in Bucharest, I had asked to purchase their old car, which they had affectionately called Nelly. She was a 1971 Chrysler Newport, dark green, with noble lines. "Big enough to play tennis in," someone remarked, and I agreed. Nelly's trunk and back seat were large enough to contain all my suitcases and air-freight baggage, that part of my old home which was to belong to my new home.

On a spring morning in late April, I said farewell to my family in Arlington, took the driver's seat in Nelly, and set out. I knew that courage consisted not in the absence of fear, but in taking action despite fear. Friends and family were praying for me that morning, but I had to take the first step—turn the key and steer, make the correct turn on to Washington Parkway, down the Beltway which would take me to Maryland and then north.

"Drive gently," it said on the Maryland State sign. Soon I was passing through the mountains of wild and wonderful West Virginia. Then due south through Kentucky. It took three days to reach the Ozarks. Sometime on the second day, as I drove alone down the turnpike in Kentucky, I felt that box into which my soul had been pressed spring open. There was a sense of freedom, the exhilarating freedom one feels before a new adventure.

I stopped at the Gateway Arch in St. Louis. The last gleams of the setting sun were reflected on the stainless steel of the giant monument which had been designed by a Finnish architect to honor the perseverance of the pioneers. They had not stopped here but continued westward. The moon was shining over the Mississippi. I walked up the steps leading to the arch, every step bringing me closer to my goal. It's true, I thought, it's climbing all the way. I just have to keep going. There are many open doors, but I don't have to go through all of them, only the ones he has chosen.

I was on my way home, back to my roots. According to author Willa Cather, roots are to be found where you have spent your childhood, especially those years between four and fourteen. For me that had been on the homestead, just outside of Springfield, Missouri. In all my travels, I had counted that place as the center of the world and had measured distance by how far away I was from my Ozarkian hills.

I am home! He has kept my going out and my coming in as is his promise in Psalm 121. And he has brought me to "a spacious place" (Ps 66:12). I am protected by the sturdy, unhewn, stone walls of my house. Outside my window I can see the strong oaks; one of them is estimated to be 250 years old. There is a special linden tree, just like the one I admired so often in Salzburg. There are maple trees of all sizes and shapes. Each tree reminds me that I must now have patience in the transplanting process for myself so that my roots will take hold in the new soil.

My faithful friends, the Getahuns write: "You are building new roots. Be patient. Take the promise of Jeremiah 24:6, "I will set my eyes upon [Ingrid] for good, and I will bring [her] back to this land, I will build [her] up, and not tear [her] down; I will plant [her], and not uproot [her]."

I am reminded of a story I once heard about a traveler in the desert. For some reason, this traveler was a very bitter man. He hated everything that was young and beautiful. One day, on the edge of an oasis, he discovered a young palm tree growing up straight and lovely. In order to cripple the tree and destroy its beauty, he fastened a heavy stone to the crown of the tree. No matter how hard the young tree tried, it could not shake off this stone. Again and again, as it attempted without success to get rid of this heavey burden, its roots thrust down deeper and deeper. They went down so deep that they soon reached the groundwater of the oasis. In spite of the burden of the rock, the palm grew up to be tall and stately. When the desert traveler passed by again, he wanted to see what he thought he had destroyed. Instead, the queenly palm bowed down to him a little and showed him the stone. "I have to thank you," it said. "You have made me strong."

So it is in our lives. That heavy stone which threatens our very existence can be the burden which causes our roots to go deeper and find the living water. Here, as I make a new beginning, with my old trunk as a symbol of all that has gone before, my prayer is that of Gerard Manley Hopkins: "O thou Lord of Life, send my roots rain."

The family is gathered shortly before Walter's death. Starting at left is Daniel, Ingrid, David, Ruth, Stephen, and Walter. Seated in front are Katrine Trobisch Stewart, David Stewart, and Christine Stewart, our first grandchild.

Afterword

JUST AS I WAS READY TO WRITE the final draft of this book, I was involved in an automobile accident. As I drove over a steep hill, I noticed, too late, a small red car which had come to a dead stop directly in front of me. If I swerved to the right, it would mean going over an embankment with my three passengers. If I swerved left, I would crash into the steady stream of oncoming traffic. I braked hard, but the invitable crash came.

Fortunately, none of my passengers were hurt, neither was the elderly couple in the red car. There was extensive damage to the two cars, and I had broken my sternum—evidently from the sudden jerk of my seatbelt, for I had not touched the steering wheel and the windshield remained unbroken.

My recovery took several weeks. The pain was great those first days, and I felt as if both heart and lungs had been loosened from their accustomed place. I couldn't even move without help.

As I look back on the accident, I realize that it is a parable in miniature of the life-changing blow I received over five years ago.

Walter and I were so thankful that we had climbed together that steep hill of our last trip across the world. Then, as we came over the crest of the hill, his heart stopped.

My whole world stopped the day Walter died, and this story is about how I learned to walk again alone. The same rules have applied as they did after my accident: Just as the doctors and nurses took care of me in the hospital, so I needed a nurturing and supporting "circle of lovers"—family and friends who made themselves available, especially in those early stages of grief, when I was incapable of walking alone.

But when the mourning is over—what then? How do you live? None of us have unlimited time, I had learned after Walter's death. Now God had underlined this truth again. I can take nothing for granted.

The words "Do it now!" have new significance. "If I have something to do, I just do it," said a wise woman. There is a fine line between doing the work which is at hand without letting it be deformed by pressure. I want to enjoy living in the moment. If I am running breathlessly here and there, I may just miss the flowering which comes in the afternoon of life.

"I know the plans I have for you, plans for good and not for evil, to give you a future and a hope." A great part of that future and hope are the four grandsons God has given me since he took away my husband. Each one reminds me in some way of their grandfather Walter—those mischievous blue eyes, the deep dimple in the chin, an inner contentedness. Life has continuity through the lives of my children and grandchildren.

Yet the battles continue. "It's not my day-battles, but my night-battles which disturb me," Martin Luther once said. I have learned not to wrestle with my own darkness, but to turn away from it to the Light.

My body and soul are the temple of his Holy Spirit. It is his will that my life should reflect the radiance of his love and my whole being repose in his peace. Only then am I able to walk alone again.

Other Books of Interest

The Facts about Your Feelings
What Every Christian Woman Should Know
Therese Cirner
Encouragement and wisdom to help you understand, control, and creatively channel your strongest emotions. A lifelong resource. Excellent for personal use and for use in small groups. $4.95

Love Has a Price Tag
Elisabeth Elliot
Encouragement, wit, and sage advice from one of today's outstanding Christian women to help you appreciate the joys *and* the trials of a life given fully to Christ. $5.95

The Open Secret
Hannah Whitall Smith
This classic devotional has helped thousands of men and women discover the Bible's secret to loving God and faithfully following him in a joy-filled life. $5.95

Available at your Christian bookstore or from
Servant • Dept. 209 • P.O. Box 7455 • Ann Arbor, MI 48107
Please include payment plus $.75 per book for postage and handling
Send for your FREE catalog of Christian books, music, and cassettes.